USDA

United States
Department of
Agriculture

Forest Service

Pacific Northwest
Research Station

General Technical Report
PNW-GTR-865

June 2012

Evaluating Tradeoffs Among Ecosystem Services in the Management of Public Lands

Jeffrey D. Kline and Marisa J. Mazzotta

Authors

Jeffrey D. Kline is a research forester, U.S. Department of Agriculture, Forest Service, Pacific Northwest Research Station, Forestry Sciences Laboratory, 3200 SW Jefferson Way, Corvallis, OR 97331; and **Marisa J. Mazzotta** is an environmental and resource economist, U.S. Environmental Protection Agency, Atlantic Ecology Division, 27 Tarzwell Drive, Narragansett, RI 02882.

Cover photo by Tom Iraci.

Abstract

Kline, Jeffrey D.; Mazzotta, Marisa J. 2012. Evaluating tradeoffs among
ecosystem services in the management of public lands. Gen. Tech. Rep. PNW-
GTR-865. Portland, OR: U.S. Department of Agriculture, Forest Service, Pacific
Northwest Research Station. 48 p.

The U.S. Forest Service has adopted the concept and language of ecosystem
services to describe the beneficial outcomes of national forest management. We
review the economic theory of ecosystem services as it applies to public lands
management, and consider what it implies about the types of biophysical and
other data that are needed for characterizing management outcomes as changes in
ecosystem services. Our intent is to provide a guide to policymakers, managers,
researchers, and others for evaluating and describing the tradeoffs involved in the
management of public lands. Characterizing ecosystem services fundamentally is
about explaining the benefits of national forests to the American public, with an
emphasis on addressing their interests and concerns about how public lands are
managed. Our hope is that this report will foster dialog about what people value
about national forests and how public land management agencies might best go
about securing those benefits.

Keywords: Ecosystem services, landscape analysis, public benefits, nonmarket
values, national forest planning and management.

Contents

"Tradeoff—a balancing of factors all of which are not attainable at the same time" (Webster's Ninth New Collegiate Dictionary 1990).

Introduction

All choices involve tradeoffs. Consider, for example, dessert. There may be times when we want to have our cake and eat it too, but by choosing cake we also choose not to have, say, pie. Choosing to have one thing now—like cake—almost always entails accepting that we cannot have another thing now—like pie. There also is the matter of the later trip to the dentist, which could involve additional conditions that we must accept in the future. That brings up the issue of time. What we choose in the present may influence the range of choices available to us or others in the future. If choosing cake today means that tomorrow the pie shop goes out of business, tomorrow we may not have the opportunity to choose between cake and pie. Choices also almost always involve some uncertainty. Which will taste better, the cake or the pie? And how likely is the pie shop to close? Lastly, choices can be difficult when they must satisfy many. If ordering dessert for a group, we may not agree amongst ourselves about which might be better, the cake or the pie. Do we vote; flip a coin? Such is the nature of everyday choices, such as those involving what car to buy, what college to attend, where to go for dinner, and what to have for dessert.

Managing public lands also involves tradeoffs. Choices about whether, where, and when to harvest timber, thin, graze, reserve, or burn—all involve tradeoffs among numerous factors that differ across landscapes and over time. They have consequences that are desirable to some and undesirable to others; and, reasonable people will disagree about the likelihood of particular consequences. Sometimes there will be sufficient information with which to describe and weigh all of the relevant factors that characterize a choice, but many choices will be fraught with missing information. The political context in which public lands management decisions are made also is complex. Some people will support proposed actions, some people will oppose, and some will oppose no matter what the intended consequences. Forest managers often express the sentiment: "We just want to manage without getting sued." How can an agency charged with managing public lands go about making sound management choices that garner public acceptance or approval? We believe that it begins with an understanding of how tradeoffs are evaluated, and an appreciation of the limitations of scientific information to support evaluating tradeoffs. Addressing those two issues is the purpose of this report.

The U.S. Forest Service has adopted the concept and language of ecosystem services to describe the beneficial outcomes of national forest management (e.g., USDA FS 2012). Ecosystem services are the services produced by forest

The concept of ecosystem services fundamentally is about explaining the benefits of national forests to the American public.

ecosystems that people enjoy or benefit from, including scenic views, fish and wildlife, clean water, and timber, to name a few. A hope is that the language of ecosystem services will help national forest managers to (1) better articulate to the public and stakeholders the benefits that national forests provide to the American public, (2) foster public support for particular management actions that might otherwise be subject to legal challenge by various groups, and (3) persuade entities who benefit from particular services (e.g., water supply for cities, trails for recreation groups) to assist in carrying out projects on national forests to enhance forest stewardship (Smith et al. 2011). Ideally, an ecosystem services framework could foster these goals by providing a means for evaluating and describing the beneficial outcomes of national forest management. The framework would provide a benefit structure for articulating forest planning goals, as well as define specific benefits that could be measured and evaluated to support project-level planning and implementation. It is a worthy goal and one that calls for a shared conceptual understanding of tradeoffs in landscape management and pragmatism about what information might be useful for describing them.

In this report, we review the economic theory of tradeoffs as it applies to public lands management and ecosystem services, and consider what it implies about the types of biophysical and other data that are needed for characterizing management outcomes as changes in ecosystem services. Our intent is to provide a guide to policymakers, managers, researchers, and others for evaluating and describing the tradeoffs inherent in the management of public lands. Characterizing ecosystem services fundamentally is about explaining the benefits of national forests to the American public, with an emphasis on addressing their interests and concerns about how national forests are managed. Our hope is that this report will foster dialog about what people value about national forests and how public land management agencies might best go about securing those benefits.

National Forest Management

Forest management has long recognized the need to consider an array of forest uses and values. As early as 1864—before creation of the National Forest System—George Perkins Marsh warned of adverse environmental effects from land clearing and noted various "services" that forests provide to people (Marsh 1864: 87, 91, 95, 232). The original mission of the Forest Service focused on protecting water and timber. But with demands soaring after World War II, the Forest Service emerged as a primary supplier of natural resource commodities, including timber and rangeland for grazing livestock (USDA FS 2005). Public demand for outdoor recreation also grew with highway improvements, increasing car ownership, and a shift away from agrarian lifestyles, among other factors. Continuing socioeconomic changes and legislation passed during the 1960s, 1970s, and 1980s broadened the Forest Service mission to include an even greater array of public benefits (Apple 2000, MacCleery 1993, MacCleery and LeMaster 1999). Key legislation included the Multiple Use Sustained Yield Act of 1960, which introduced multiple-use management, and the National Forest Management Act of 1976, which incorporated multiple-use management into forest planning. Nonmarket benefits grew in stature to rival commodity (or market) values as a management focus. Multiple-use management eventually evolved to incorporate ecosystem management—formally adopted by the Forest Service in 1992 (Thomas 1996, USDA FS 1992). Whereas multiple-use management tended to focus on landscape **outputs**—cubic feet of timber, animal unit months of grazing, or recreation days, for example—ecosystem management focused more on landscape **conditions**, with outputs more often viewed as byproducts of meeting ecosystem objectives (Grumbine 1994, Kaufmann et al. 1994, MacLeary and LeMaster 1999). Ecosystem management also broadened the management perspective to consider social and ecological interactions over a variety of spatial and temporal scales, rather than outputs produced at a single time and place (MacLeary and LeMaster 1999).

The evolving need to consider a wider array of benefits has made managing national forests more complex. It has expanded the amount of information required for characterizing management effects and increased the level of scrutiny that national forests receive from the public and nongovernmental organizations. Earnest research efforts by the Forest Service and others have developed and improved methods for weighing multiple forest benefits, but have not eased the complexity (text box 1). At the same time, there has been increasing recognition that many forest benefits derive from landscape conditions and processes that transcend national forest boundaries. For landscape management to effectively provide desired forest benefits, it must consider the role of all lands—public and private—when devising management activities and evaluating their likely outcomes. This "all lands" perspective broadens the geographic scope over which forest benefits and the landscape conditions and processes on which they depend might be evaluated.

National forest management as currently conducted involves (1) forest planning, which involves developing broad and long-term landscape objectives; and (2) project-level planning and implementation, which involves developing and executing individual local projects that pursue objectives outlined in the forest plan. The National Environmental Policy Act of 1970 requires managers to assess the environmental effects of any ground-disturbing project proposed. Individuals or interest groups use litigation under the Administrative Procedure Act (1966) and the Appeals Reform Act (1992) to ensure that their particular concerns are addressed in

Text box 1: The Forest Service and research pertaining to ecosystem services

The recent interest in ecosystem services within the Forest Service continues a line of scientific inquiry pertaining to the public benefits of national forest management. In forestry, the roots of such inquiry arguably extend back decades to work by Gregory (1955), who applied traditional production economics theory to forestry to define multiple-use management as a problem of joint production of multiple outputs. Gregory (1955) focused on those forest outputs of interest at the time, including timber, forage, water, recreation, and habitat for species of commercial or recreational interest. Building on Gregory were other works on multiple-use forestry, including Pearse (1969), O'Connell and Brown (1972), Walter (1977), Alston (1979), and Teeguarden (1982), to name a few. However, the National Forest Management Act (1976) mandated that the forest managers address a wider array of forest benefits and values, including nonmarket benefits, in their analyses of proposed projects. This ushered in a period of especially intensive research effort among environmental and resource economists, focused on describing nonmarket values associated with the management of public forests.

Of particular importance is the work of John Krutilla at Resources for the Future, whose work on the economics of public forest lands was funded in part by the Forest Service during the 1970s as the agency sought to define "a rational basis for multiple-use" (Buckman 2010). In previous work, Krutilla had noted the importance of "providing for the present and future the amenities associated with unspoiled natural environments, for which the market fails to make adequate provision" (Krutilla 1967: 778). Krutilla provided economic reasoning for why nonmarketed natural resources had economic value, and why the opportunity costs of protecting natural resources and their services should be considered and compared to extractive-use values. He was one of the first economists to propose an approach to measuring nonmarket values (Resources for the Future 2003). Up to that time, the service flows provided by natural environments were typically relegated to the category of intangibles and did not play a meaningful role in economic analysis (Flores 2002: 3). Krutilla's efforts for the Forest Service eventually formed the foundation for the widely cited *Multiple-Use Management: The Economics of Public Forest Lands*, by Bowes and Krutilla (1989).

(continued on next page)

> Bowes and Krutilla (1989) noted two key informational needs: (1) characterizing the responses of vegetation and wildlife to management, and (2) the economic valuation of biophysical products (e.g., ecosystem services). In response, much of the economics research in forestry throughout the 1980s to the present has focused on valuing the nonmarket benefits of ecosystem services provided by forests, to support management decisions. These efforts are exemplified in works such as *Valuation of Wildland Resource Benefits* by Peterson and Randall (1984), and *Amenity Resource Valuation* by Peterson et al. (1988). These and other works also have involved Forest Service funding and scientists. This work continues within the agency today, with examples such as *A Primer on Nonmarket Valuation*, by Champ et al. (2003). Although much progress has been made in evaluating ecosystem services, the informational challenges identified by Bowes and Krutilla (1989) remain as the greatest obstacles to applying the ecosystem services framework to national forest management. It is now increasingly recognized that further progress requires multidisciplinary and interdisciplinary approaches.

assessments conducted to support forest planning and individual projects. Frequent use of litigation by various interest groups has led to many proposed projects now taking years to litigate and then implement, assuming they survive litigation. From the Forest Service perspective, these changes have resulted in a management process that impedes the ability of national forests to complete needed work in a timely manner—work that is viewed as necessary to fulfill the Forest Service's own ecosystem restoration objectives.

A factor that may have increased the likelihood of litigation is the Forest Service's own reporting and reward requirements, which have focused on accomplishing functional targets assigned by Congress. Examples of targets include cubic feet of timber produced and sold, amount of firewood offered, miles of road constructed or decommissioned, acres of forest fire fuels reduced, and annual unit-months of grazing permits awarded (Smith et al. 2011). For some observers, the focus on functional targets has tended to obscure the degree to which managers actually consider a full array of forest benefits in planning and project-level decision processes. The lack of integrated assessment, whether real or perceived, conceivably fostered distrust among particular nongovernment organizations and the public about whether the Forest Service adequately considered all factors affected by proposed management actions. Some national forest policymakers and managers speculate that the

A hope is that the concept and language of ecosystem services will enable the agency to present a stronger rationale for forest planning goals and specific projects that are planned and implemented.

focus on functional targets and associated distrust made litigation over proposed projects all the more likely.

Interest in including ecosystem services concepts and language into national forest management arises in part from the Forest Service's recognition that management processes may not always have provided a sufficient accounting of public benefits. A hope is that the concept and language of ecosystem services will enable the agency to present a stronger rationale for forest planning goals and specific projects that are planned and implemented, by outlining a more inclusive set of benefits as outcomes of management. Ideally, these changes, combined with an open and meaningful public participatory process, will make national forest management more understandable and less contentious. It is a worthy goal; however, introduction of an ecosystem services framework into national forest management does not necessarily ease the work of weighing and characterizing the tradeoffs associated with proposed plans and projects. That task still depends on managers being able to characterize likely changes in landscape conditions and processes, and associated ecosystem services, as expected outcomes of management in ways that people can understand and trust. That always has been, and still is, the challenge.

Forest planning is the appropriate avenue for incorporating the concept and language of ecosystem services into national forest management. Forest plans provide the broad goals and objectives that guide management by describing desired future conditions for national forests. Forest plan goals should be stated in terms of the relevant and valued benefits provided by national forests. Project-level planning and implementation involves specific management actions at local scales, to effect movement toward the desired future conditions outlined in forest plans. Project-level planning and implementation should draw upon the benefits language provided in forest plans to describe the expected outcomes of management actions. Both the forest and project-level planning and implementation processes can be entirely consistent with an ecosystem services conceptual framing of landscape benefits. We believe that the analytical tasks involved in evaluating and characterizing ecosystem services actually are rather similar to the ways in which national forest managers have addressed multiple landscape benefits in the past. The timing, then, would seem appropriate for reviewing the economics of landscape management and its associated social benefits, in the context of ecosystem services.

An Economic Theory of Landscape Management and Tradeoffs

In a public lands management context, ecosystem services are beneficial outcomes that derive from landscape conditions (e.g., forest structure, species composition) and processes as they are altered by management (fig. 1). Each year, managers decide how to spend their allocated management budget. Managers consider existing landscape conditions in light of the broad objectives identified in the forest plan, and identify a reasonable set of management activities to pursue, whose costs fit within the allocated budget. The conceptual model includes the significant role that natural disturbance—wildfire, insects, and disease, for example—can play in influencing the types of management activities that are accomplished and the future landscape conditions managers will face. Management activities and the resulting changes they effect on the landscape, combined with vegetative growth, natural disturbances, and other landscape changes define the landscape conditions managers will face the following year (fig. 1). The process of evaluating landscape conditions relative to forest plan goals, identifying and implementing projects, and monitoring their effects continues as a cycle, repeating year after year (e.g., Kline 2004).

The social benefits and costs associated with landscape management accrue in any given year according to the landscape conditions present, management actions taken, and natural disturbances that occur (fig. 2). Landscape conditions and their spatial arrangements largely determine the types and amounts of various ecosystem services society receives. For example, vegetation, riparian conditions, and other landscape characteristics determine the quality of surface water available for human consumption. The spatial arrangements of forest structure and species composition determine habitat conditions and wildlife populations. The developed recreation infrastructure will determine the variety of recreation opportunities available. The degree to which any given ecosystem service is a benefit depends on a combination

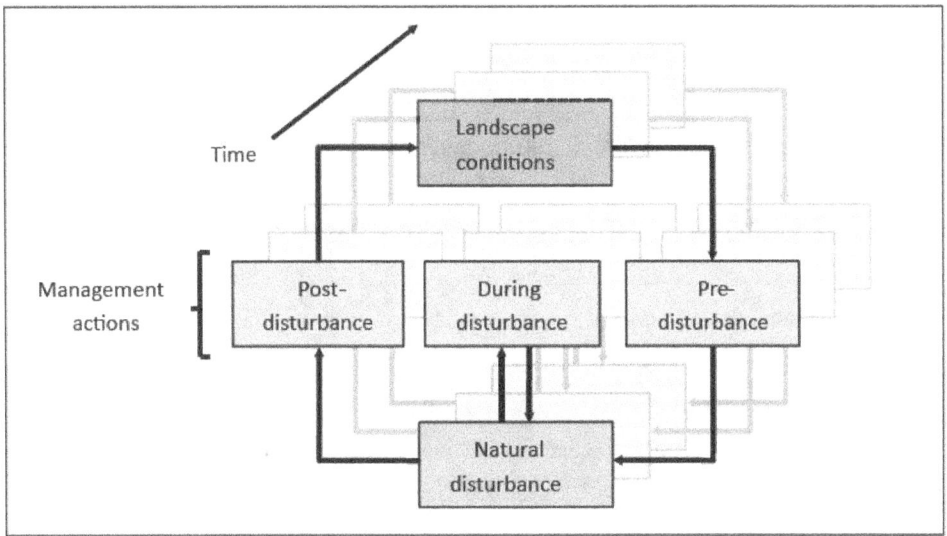

Figure 1—Conceptual model of management and disturbance influences on landscape conditions through time.

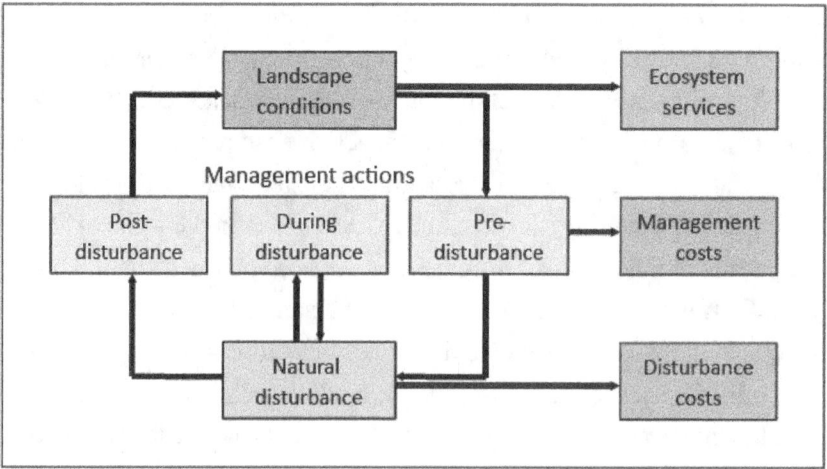

Figure 2—Benefits and costs associated with landscapes, management, and disturbance in a given year.

In a public lands management context, ecosystem services are beneficial outcomes that derive from landscape conditions and processes as they are altered by management.

of factors, including how scarce it is, how accessible it is to people, how much it is valued by people, and by how many people it is valued.

Management actions produce costs associated with the planning, labor, and equipment used to implement projects (fig. 2). Natural disturbances that occur produce additional costs associated with, for example, smoke, property damage, and suppression in the case of wildfire. Any ecological damages—or reduced flows of ecosystem services resulting from natural disturbance or management—are reflected in altered landscape conditions and associated declines in ecosystem services in future years. The whole process takes place in the larger context of climate and climate change, which can alter landscape and natural disturbance processes and the influence that management might have on them (e.g., Kline 2004).

The forest landscape thus exists as a stock of natural capital with a capacity to produce flows of ecosystem services over time. Landscape conditions at any point in time determine the type, quality, and quantity of the ecosystem services produced, and the potential benefits that people receive. Managers decide how best to influence landscape conditions through management, with consequent changes in ecosystem services. The value of the ecosystem services produced from the landscape, less management costs and costs associated with any natural disturbances, make up the net social benefit or economic return that the landscape provides to the public in a given year. Although ecosystem services include benefits not typically expressed by people in terms of dollars, such as aesthetics, wildlife, and various recreational experiences, these "nonmarket benefits" are no less important to the economic evaluation of forest management actions than benefits for which values can more easily be expressed in terms of dollars, such as timber and grazing. The economics of landscape management in a public lands context is about reflecting the variety of benefits that people perceive from landscapes to inform policy and management decisions in pursuit of the greatest good. If a particular ecosystem service is of interest to people, then it is of economic interest to managers.

Flows of ecosystem services are not constant, but rather fluctuate over time according to changing landscape conditions. Managers largely plan and implement projects in the present to manipulate landscape conditions, and thereby effect changes in flows of ecosystem services in the future. In this way, each management action taken or not taken contributes to defining an ecological trajectory of landscape conditions and associated ecosystem services over time (fig. 3). This trajectory is initiated by a management action and subsequently influenced by effected changes in forest structure and species composition in years following a management action, and any influences those actions might have on natural disturbance processes.

For example, consider a landscape featuring a fixed network of hiking trails that attracts a known level of use measured in hiking days (fig. 4a). In the absence of any management action, managers might expect the level of hiking days to remain fairly constant from year to year. Now suppose managers decide to increase the recreation capacity of an existing trail network by adding a new trail. This might be expected to draw greater numbers of users, resulting in an expected increase in

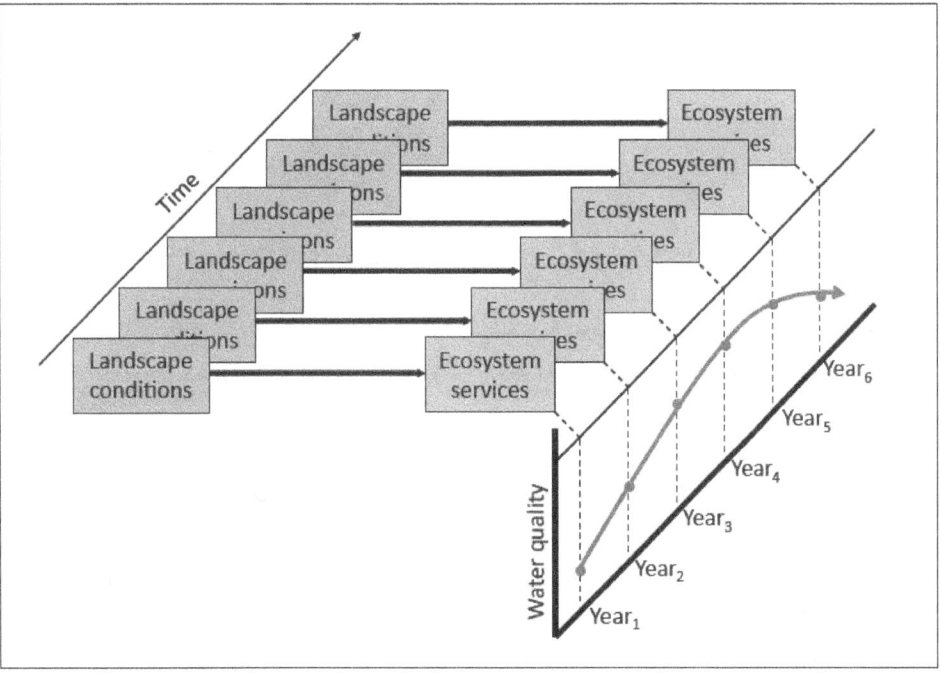

Figure 3—Landscape conditions and associated ecosystem services trajectory through time—water quality as an example.

hiking days (fig. 4a). Conversely, perhaps an alternative plan would increase timber harvesting. Managers might consider a harvest visible from a large proportion of the hiking trails in the trail network (fig. 4b). The proposed harvest reasonably might be expected to displace would-be hikers, who may choose to hike elsewhere, because the trail network might be perceived as less scenic than it was before the harvest. The result might be an initial decline in hiking days with gradual recovery over time with sufficient regrowth of forest vegetation (fig. 4b).

Other time trajectories will exist for other ecosystem services as they might be influenced by proposed management actions. For example, managers might consider excluding livestock from a particular stream corridor to reduce soil compaction and erosion, enable riparian vegetation to recover, and improve water quality (fig. 4c). Managers might decide to address declines in a local elk population by selectively harvesting several forest stands to improve their forage value (fig 4d).

Similar to the influence of management actions, changing landscape conditions and especially natural disturbances, such as wildfires, insects, and disease, also will contribute to defining the manner in which flows of ecosystem services differ from year to year. Consider again our hiking example, where in the absence of any

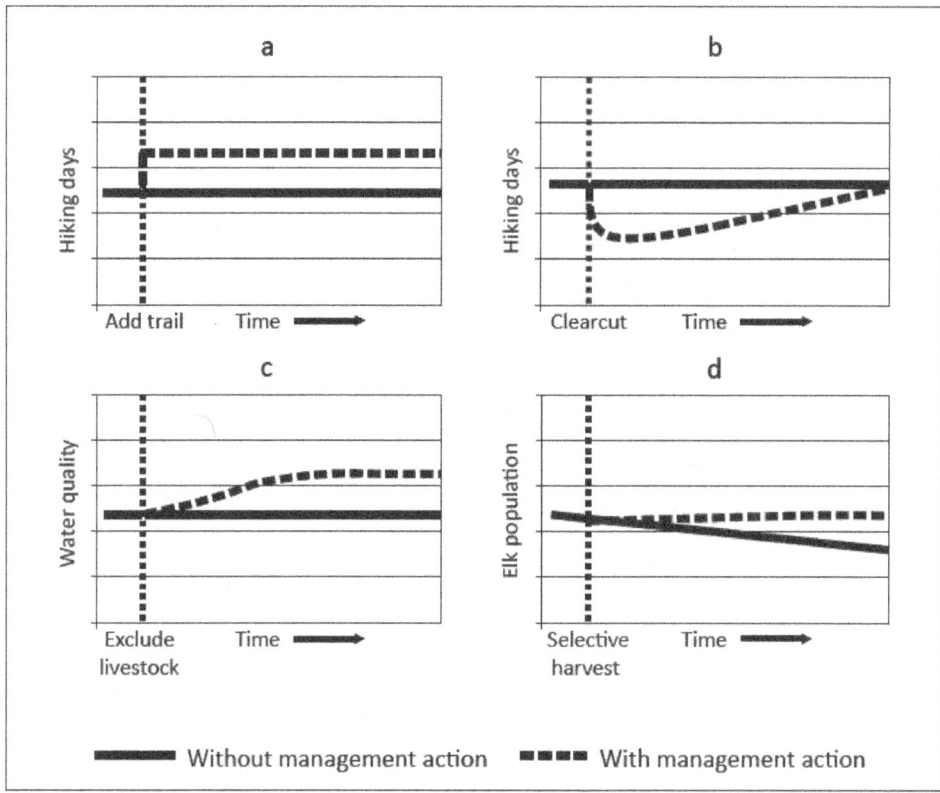

Figure 4—Hypothetical expected ecosystem services trajectories with and without specific management actions: (a) hiking days with new trail, (b) hiking days with clearcut, (c) water quality with livestock exclusion, and (d) elk population with selective harvest.

management action, managers might expect the level of hiking days to remain fairly constant from year to year (fig. 5a). Now suppose a wildfire burns through most of the existing trail network. An initial effect might be for the entire trail network to be closed to users such that hiking days are dramatically reduced (fig. 5a). However, during the first few years following the wildfire, perhaps a profusion of wildflowers draws increasing numbers of hikers attracted to the new scenery. Others may also be attracted by the wildfire event itself, curious to witness the degree of destruction. In ensuing years, perhaps hiking again declines as the young tree cover of the recovering forest offers little in the way of scenic views. Eventually, as the trees mature, hiking days may fully rebound to their prewildfire level.

Other time trajectories will exist for other landscape conditions and ecosystem services. For example, grazing units might initially decline owing to temporary closure of the area, but quickly increase as forage thrives on the burned landscape (fig. 5b). Woodpecker populations might increase with the growing numbers of snags, then decline as snags collapse (fig. 5c). Carbon storage, which had been on a gradually increasing trajectory, initially might decline, but eventually would recover with regrowth (fig. 5d).

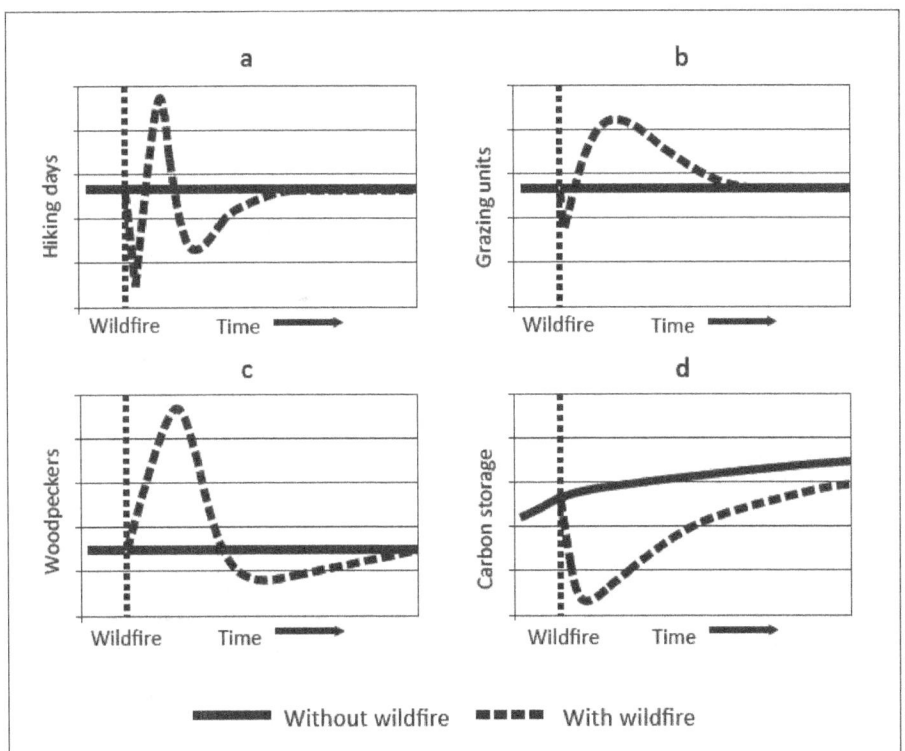

Figure 5—Hypothetical expected ecosystem services trajectories with and without wildfire: (a) hiking days with wildfire, (b) grazing units with wildfire, (c) woodpeckers with wildfire, and (d) carbon storage with wildfire.

Evaluating and communicating the potential benefits that managers expect from any given management action ideally would include information describing the expected time trajectories of valued ecosystem services as they are altered by management.

Evaluating and communicating the potential benefits that managers expect from any given management action ideally would include information describing the expected time trajectories of valued ecosystem services as they are altered by management, combined with some measure of the degree to which those services are valued by people. The actual path that different ecosystem services might take typically will not be known with certainty. Natural disturbances as well as variation in climatic conditions that affect vegetative growth will ensure some unpredictability. At best, managers may be able to anticipate a set of confidence bounds defining the range of values over which the true path might stray. Conceivably, these confidence bounds widen through time reflecting greater error in predictions made further into the future (fig. 6). An implication of widening confidence bounds is that future ecosystem services trajectories that managers might expect to result from different proposed management actions may at times overlap such that the distinction between the expected outcomes of two different alternatives might be cloudy at best (fig. 7). Such circumstances call for describing the degree of confidence that managers have in their expectations of management outcomes, including the degree to which one outcome is likely to differ from another. Any characterization of expected time trajectories should include some representation of the level of confidence that managers have in predictions (e.g., confidence bounds), as well as an indication of uncertainty associated with potential natural disturbances. Under

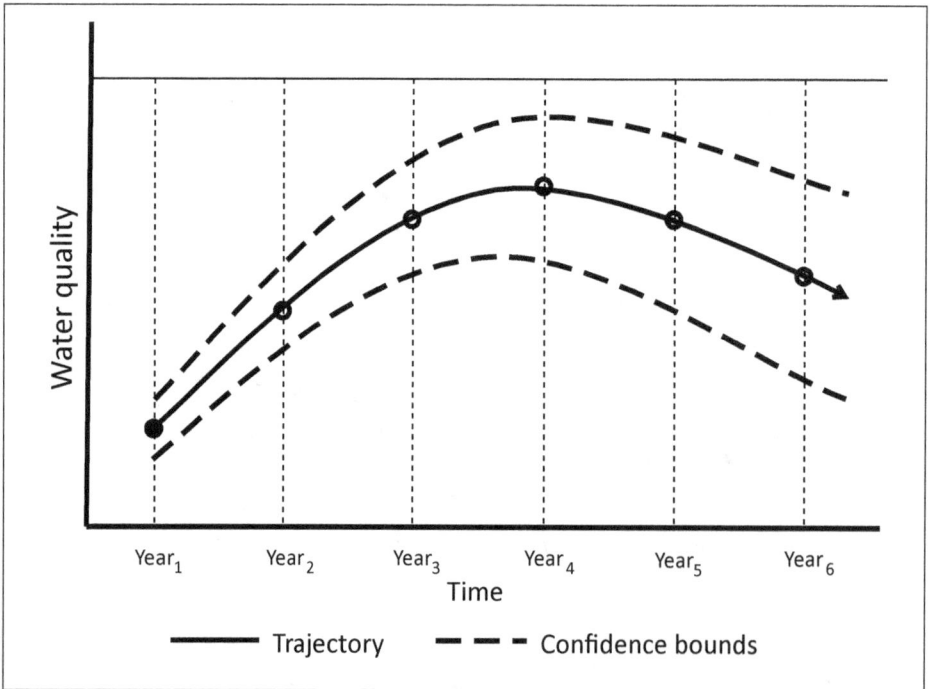

Figure 6—Example of expected ecosystem services trajectory showing expanding confidence bounds through time.

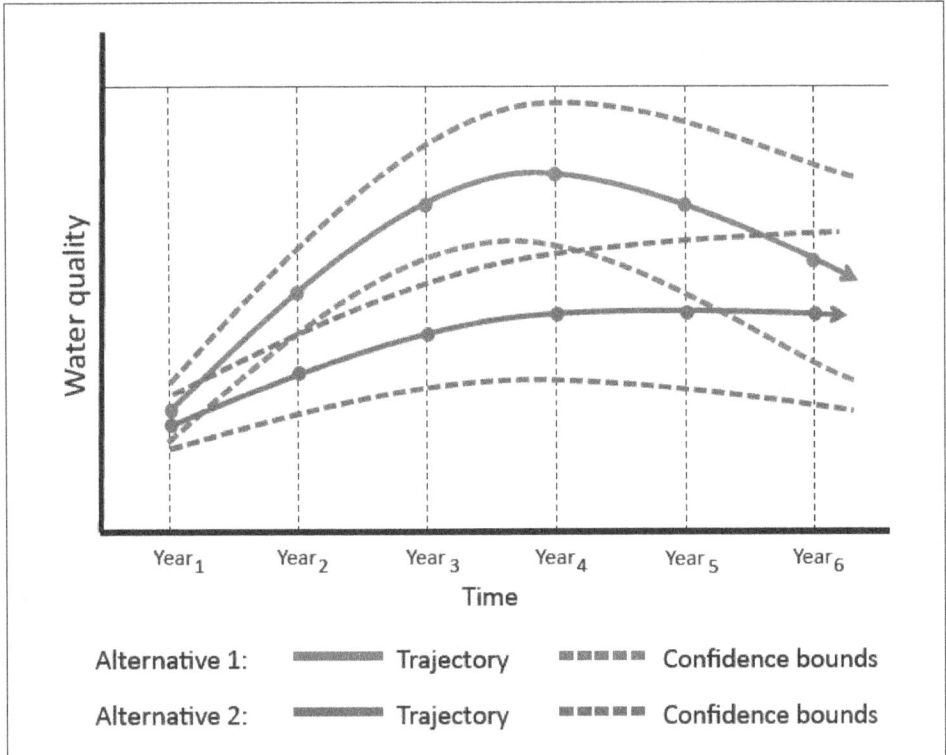

Figure 7—Two expected ecosystem services trajectories resulting from two difference management alternatives, showing overlap of expanding confidence bounds through time.

adaptive management, these trajectories would be reestimated periodically, to enable adjustments to management as events on the landscape unfold.

Tradeoffs

National forests can be viewed as striving to produce a "portfolio" of ecosystem services to provide the greatest overall benefit to the public within a landscape's capacity to produce services, and within any necessary safe minimum standards, mandated institutional constraints, and legal requirements (e.g., the Endangered Species Act). National forest plans define the portfolio of services a national forest will strive for, by outlining the broad- and long-term objectives for the managed landscape. Project-level planning and implementation pursues management activities in accordance with forest plans to enhance flows of particular ecosystem services—to improve a specific fish or wildlife population, for example, or reduce the likelihood that natural disturbance (e.g., wildfire) might adversely affect flows of ecosystem services. However, many ecosystem services and the associated landscape conditions from which they derive are interrelated in either conflicting or synergistic ways such that changes in one service necessarily involve changes in another service. In some cases, increased flows of one service may only be possible by accepting decreased flows of another service. Evaluating and communicating expected management outcomes necessarily must account for these interrelationships and the tradeoffs—the exchange of one level of service for another—made necessary when implementing a project that will affect multiple ecosystem service flows.

Conceptually, tradeoffs among ecosystem services are best illustrated by using the economic concept of "production possibility frontiers" (e.g., Bowes and Krutilla 1989: 49, Stevens and Montgomery 2002). Production possibility frontiers show the combinations and levels of ecosystem services that can be produced on a landscape given that landscape's capacity to produce those services (e.g., its size and biophysical features) and management inputs (e.g., labor) and capital improvements (e.g., roads, trails, culverts). The "landscape" can be a national forest or a ranger district or a larger area encompassing a national forest and neighboring lands, depending on what makes sense for characterizing a given set of ecosystem services and their management. In either case, production possibility frontiers combine the relationships that characterize the production of individual ecosystem services in terms of

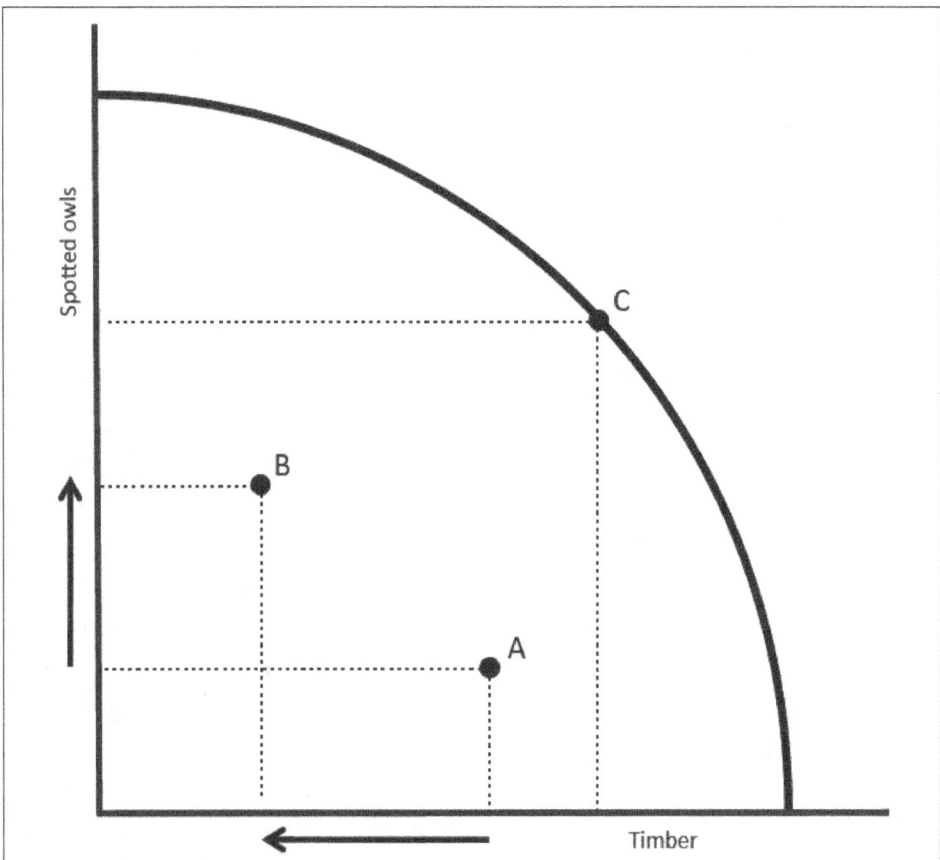

Figure 8—Example of the joint production possibilities choice set expected from select management alternatives.

specific landscape conditions and processes to describe how the production of one ecosystem service relates to production of another service.

Consider two ecosystem services that can be thought of as competitive in production. For example, producing merchantable timber can be considered competitive with production of spotted owls. We will assume that timber production is a positive function of land and site quality and is best served by managing forest stands on shorter rotations, such that it is negatively related to amount of land devoted to the old-growth habitat preferred by spotted owls. Under these assumptions, a forest landscape can only produce so many spotted owls and so much timber, up to some limit at which the production of owls can only be increased by decreasing the production of timber. That limit is the production possibility frontier (fig. 8). The production possibility frontier defines the range of combinations of jointly produced ecosystem services (e.g., owls and timber) given a set of inputs—inputs in this case being the fixed landscape and the management budget. We can produce any combinations of owls and timber inside the frontier (e.g., points A and B) as well as any combinations on the frontier itself (e.g. point C). However, once on the frontier, we can only produce more owls by producing less timber or more timber by producing fewer owls—hence the need to make tradeoffs among services produced on the landscape, by exchanging timber for owls or owls for timber.

The feasible points within the area defined by the production possibility frontier identify the levels of services associated with different management regimes. Comparing the service levels of two different management regimes identifies the tradeoffs associated with choosing one regime over another. For example, if the management regime associated with service levels defined by point B were chosen over the status quo regime defined by point A, managers could expect less timber and more owls as a result—trading off (or exchanging) timber for owls (fig. 8). Understanding the production possibilities for a given landscape enables managers to identify and weigh the possible output combinations that might be expected on a given landscape, and may make it more feasible to avoid unnecessary tradeoffs. For example, suppose the public wanted to avoid having to give up timber production in exchange for gains in spotted owls that the move from point A to point B entails. If managers had adequate information about the full range of production possibilities available on the landscape, they could instead strive for a management regime closer to that defined by point C that would yield increases in both timber and spotted owls.

Better outcomes typically are those that enable greater production of both services or of one service without giving up any other, and ideally by moving from any interior point to a point on the frontier itself. Shifting to better outcomes may only be feasible through judicious application of management over long time periods. Ideally, management actions would pursue improvements in desired ecosystem services over time. That is, managers would seek to initiate ecological time trajectories that move outcomes from interior positions out toward the production possibilities frontier (fig. 9). However, identifying management actions with which to move landscape conditions toward those better outcomes relies on having good information about what ecosystem services combinations are possible and what management actions would bring them about. These conditions may not always exist.

An important characteristic of production possibility frontiers is that they define joint production possibilities **given existing resource endowments and inputs**. That is, the position of the frontier—the line—is based on the resource endowments and biophysical characteristics (e.g., land area, soils, topography) of the landscape under management along with inputs of labor and capital enabled by the management budget. Increases in either factor can shift the frontier outward (to the right) enabling greater joint production possibilities. For example, a land

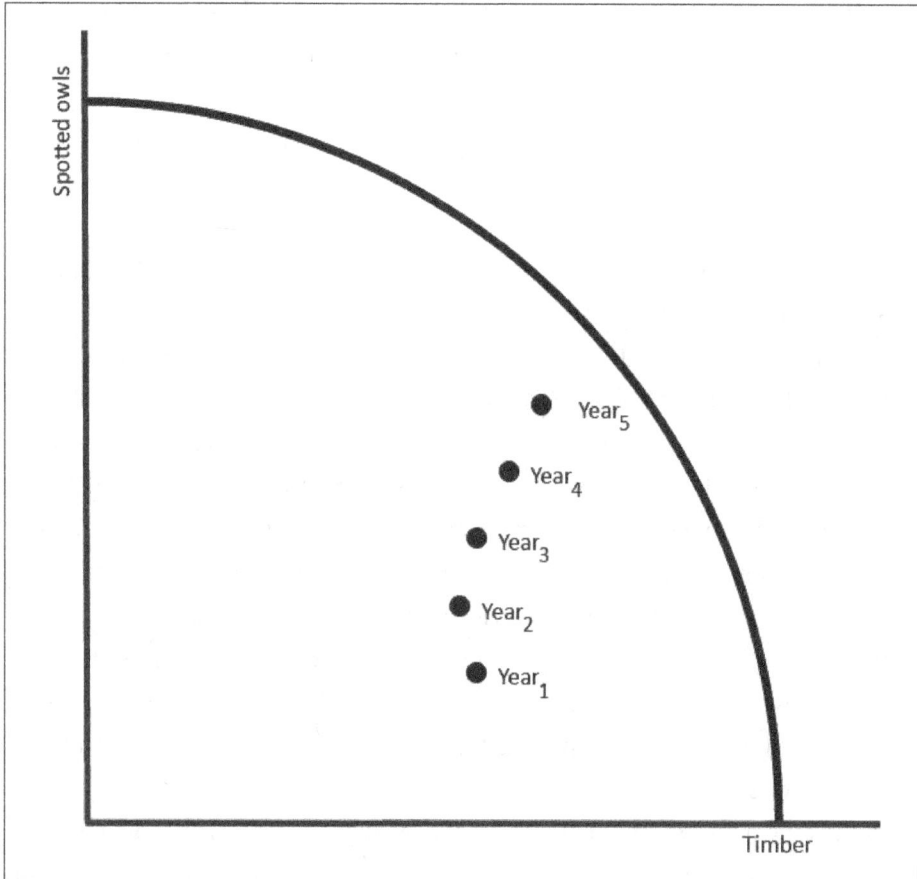

Figure 9—Hypothetical time trajectory of year-to-year improvements in ecosystem services outcomes.

management agency could increase the resource endowment by expanding the size of the managed landscape. It could purchase more land or through education and financial incentives try to persuade neighboring private landowners to manage according to a similar set of management objectives—an "all-lands" approach. Conversely, reductions in the resource endowment and inputs will tend to contract the frontier inward (to the left) toward lesser joint production possibilities. For example, if budget reductions mean that fewer hiking trails can be maintained or campgrounds staffed, that could contract inward the production possibility frontier in terms of recreation. Natural disturbances also could alter production possibilities by enhancing or damaging landscape conditions and associated ecosystem services. Conceivably, other exogenous factors—most notably changing climate—could also alter production possibilities and would factor into management considerations given a sufficiently long planning horizon.

Another characteristic of production possibility frontiers is their shape, which defines the general relationship between two ecosystem services in production (fig. 10). Competing ecosystem services are those for which more of one service can only be had at the expense of producing less of the other service. The simplest form of the production possibility frontier for two competing services is linear, denoting a constant exchange of one output for another (fig. 10a). Production possibility frontiers depicting competing services also can be convex (fig. 10b) or concave (fig. 10c) when there are nonlinear relationships between two services at the frontier. The actual shape is determined by the precise relationship between the two ecosystem services in terms of the landscape and input factors involved in their production.

The slope of the production possibility frontier at any point is the rate at which one service (x) must be given up to produce more of another service (y) when a

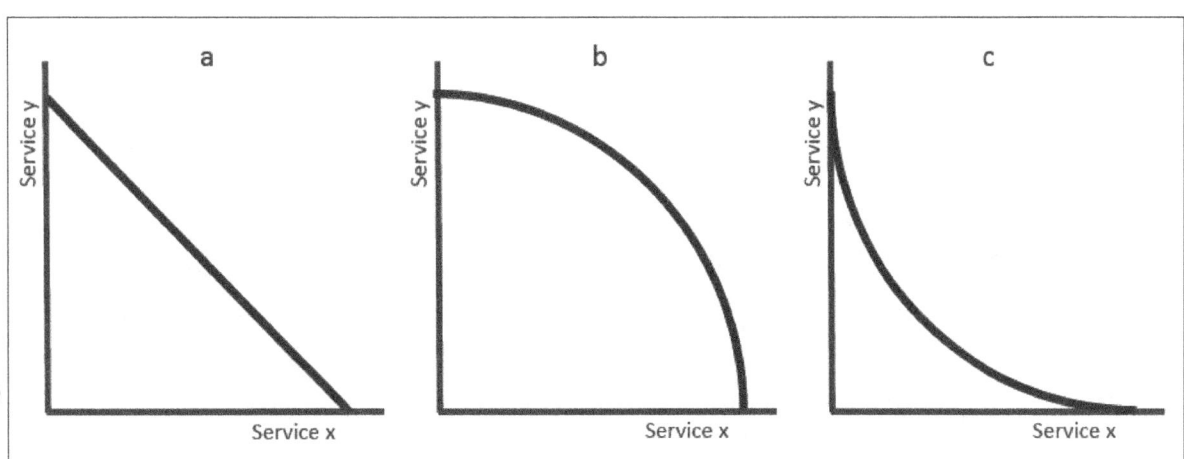

Figure 10—Possible shapes of production possibility frontiers for outputs that are competing in production: (a) linear form, (b) convex form, and (c) concave form.

landscape is producing the maximum joint production combination possible (on the frontier). The linear form (constant slope) implies that the same inputs can produce either service equally well so that, when inputs are shifted to increase one service, the quantity of the other that must be given up remains constant for all initial combinations of the two services. A convex form (fig. 10b) occurs when small increases in one service can only be had by giving up increasing amounts of another service. Economists refer to this as "diminishing marginal productivity" (e.g., Lesser et al. 1997). For example, when the initial quantity of service x is low (at a point near the y-axis), a small increase can be had by giving up a small amount of y. Conversely, when the quantity of x already is high (at a point near the x-axis) that same increase in x can only be had by giving up a much larger amount of service y (fig. 10b). Similarly, when the quantity of service y is high (at a point near the Y-axis) a given increase in y can only be had by giving up increasing amounts of service x.

The concave form (fig. 10c) implies that, as more of one service is produced, less and less of another service must be given up for each additional unit. This can be the case when the production of one service (service x in the diagram) results in an externality, or unintended negative effect, that hinders production of the other service. For example, increasing hiking trails could have a detrimental effect on wildlife habitat, by bringing more people into forest areas. As more of the service affected by the externality (e.g., wildlife habitat) is produced relative to the other service (e.g., hiking trails), increasingly smaller amounts of the other must be given up (e.g., Baumol and Bradford 1972). This occurs because decreasing production of service x will also decrease its negative effect on service y, resulting in increasing gains in y for the same change in x, as x decreases. Other complexities related to biological production and relationships between species may also lead to a concave production possibility frontier (e.g., Brown et al. 2010, Swallow et al. 1990), but are beyond the scope of this report.

Some ecosystem services are not competitive in production with others. Rather, the production of one service might coincide with (or complement) the production of another. Ecosystem services that are complementary in production occur when both ecosystem services are positively related to the same landscape conditions or processes, such as two wildlife species thriving in the same type of habitat, or when one ecosystem service depends on another as a factor in its production, such as spotted owls and old growth. Similar to competing services, the precise relationships among complementary services can be linear or nonlinear depending on the specific relationships among the two ecosystems services and the landscape and input factors involved in their production. Complementary relationships among ecosystem services generally are less of an issue when considering tradeoffs associated with management activities, because they generally do not pose potential conflicts associated with expected outcomes. You generally do not have to give up old growth to gain in spotted owls, for example. However, complementary services can be important to tradeoff analysis if one of a set of complementary services is easier to measure than the others and can thus serve as an indicator for other services for which measurement may be more difficult.

We have only considered production possibility frontiers for two ecosystem services as this is the easiest scenario to represent using simple graphics. Conceptually, one can imagine production possibility relationships for multiple services, but displaying multiple production possibility relationships quickly becomes more difficult, as does empirically estimating those relationships. In fact, it may not always be possible to characterize the inherent complexity in the production relationship among some ecosystem service combinations using relatively simple production possibility frontiers. Rather, the complexity of natural systems might more often imply complex production relationships that feature thresholds, tipping points, or other nonlinear production changes that defy characterization using simple mathematical functions. Managers often may lack sufficient information with which to accurately describe the true relationship between various ecosystem services. Gaps in knowledge about how different ecological agents and processes interact at landscape scales can make even speculating about such complex relationships controversial. Indeed, the precise position of the production possibility frontier may be largely unknown, so that management alternatives are more likely to yield ecosystem services outcomes that are inferior to production possibilities defined by the frontier itself. These are questions of ecology and necessarily call for ecological information to support the evaluation and communication of management outcomes.

Yet, lack of well-defined projections of production possibilities need not prevent managers from framing management actions and associated tradeoffs in terms of what ecosystem services are possible on a given landscape. But it does mean that any characterization of expected services must be conditioned on the degree of confidence in those expectations. Even with imperfect information, a focus on outcomes framed in the context of what ecosystem services are possible on a landscape, and how they are related, can be a useful way to focus dialog and debate. Managers have some sense of what levels of ecosystem services are possible on a given landscape and can describe how relevant ecosystem services are likely to change as a result of projects under consideration. These two conditions are all that is necessary to characterize tradeoffs among ecosystem services associated with pursuing one project or another, if only qualitatively. Ideally, analysis would be based on empirical functions that describe a suite of ecosystem services relative

Understanding the specific relationships between landscape conditions, management activities, and their influence on ecosystem services is thus an essential first step toward considering tradeoffs among services.

to the landscape conditions (or factors) that will be directly or indirectly affected by a proposed project, such as trees per acre, stand density, stand structure, or the amount of understory, for example. However, in the absence of empirical information, analysts may need to rely on a qualitative narrative or some other way of describing how proposed projects are expected to affect the relevant ecosystem services, including potential magnitude of changes in ecosystem services. Understanding the specific relationships between landscape conditions, management activities, and their influence on ecosystem services is thus an essential first step toward considering tradeoffs among services.

Social Values

The production relationships among landscape conditions and ecosystem services present only part of the tradeoff picture—the part having to do with the degree to which different combinations of ecosystem services can be produced or **supplied** on a given landscape with a given management budget. They say nothing about the social value of individual services or which combination of services might be socially preferred or **demanded** by the public. Identifying which combination of ecosystem services might be most preferred requires additional information describing the relative values that people place on different ecosystem services or the preferences they hold for particular ecosystem service combinations. This involves the issue of what people expect to gain as a return on the Nation's investment in managing national forests.

In economics, the fundamental concept of an individual's level of satisfaction or well-being is **utility**—the satisfaction that an individual expects from a given choice or course of action (e.g., Gwartney and Stroup 1980:7). For example, a hiker living near a particular national forest might perceive a level of satisfaction from the hiking trails offered by that forest. How much satisfaction conceivably might depend on the number of trails (or trail miles) offered. To use a simple example, if a forest offers only 1 mile of trail, the hiker receives one level of satisfaction. If the forest offers 2 miles of trail, the hiker likely receives a higher level of satisfaction. Hiking the same 1 mile of trail might eventually get boring, after all, and so having a second mile of trail would offer a nice change of pace. It is safe to assume then that the hiker's overall level of satisfaction—or utility—increases as a positive function of hiking trail miles (fig. 11). The increase in satisfaction associated with an incremental increase in trail miles is referred to as the hiker's marginal utility associated with an additional trail mile (e.g., Gwartney and Stroup 1980:89).

The positive relationship between trail miles and the hiker's satisfaction likely will not be constant. Rather, each trail mile added to the forest may eventually begin to yield incrementally less satisfaction such that the hiker's marginal utility

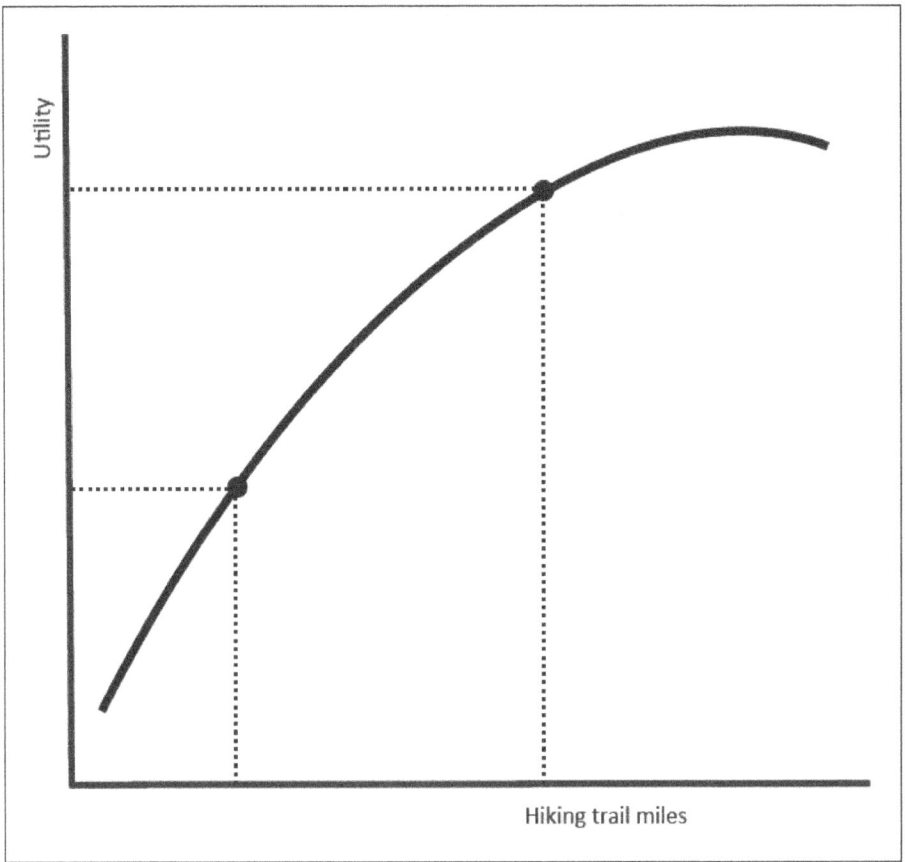

Figure 11—Example of utility (or satisfaction) of an individual with increasing number of trail miles provided by a national forest.

associated with an additional trail mile is "diminishing" (fig. 11). The hiker only has time to hike so many miles of trail, after all, and so at some point, adding an additional trail mile to the forest is unlikely to yield much increase in the hiker's overall satisfaction. Conceivably, at some point the hiker's level of satisfaction may even decline with each additional trail mile if the hiker feels that there already are too many trails and perhaps too many other hikers as a result. At some point, the hiker's marginal utility for additional trail miles can even turn negative, such that further increases in trail miles would yield lower levels of overall satisfaction for the hiker. Returning to our cake example, this would be the point at which our stomach has informed us that indeed we have eaten way too much cake.

If an individual receives an equal level of utility from different combinations of the same two ecosystem services, that person can be said to be indifferent as to which is preferred. This equality in satisfaction can be represented by an indifference curve (fig. 12). Consider, for example, an individual who enjoys both hiking and fishing, and therefore receives utility from both hiking trails and trout streams. The national forest near where this individual lives provides both hiking trails and

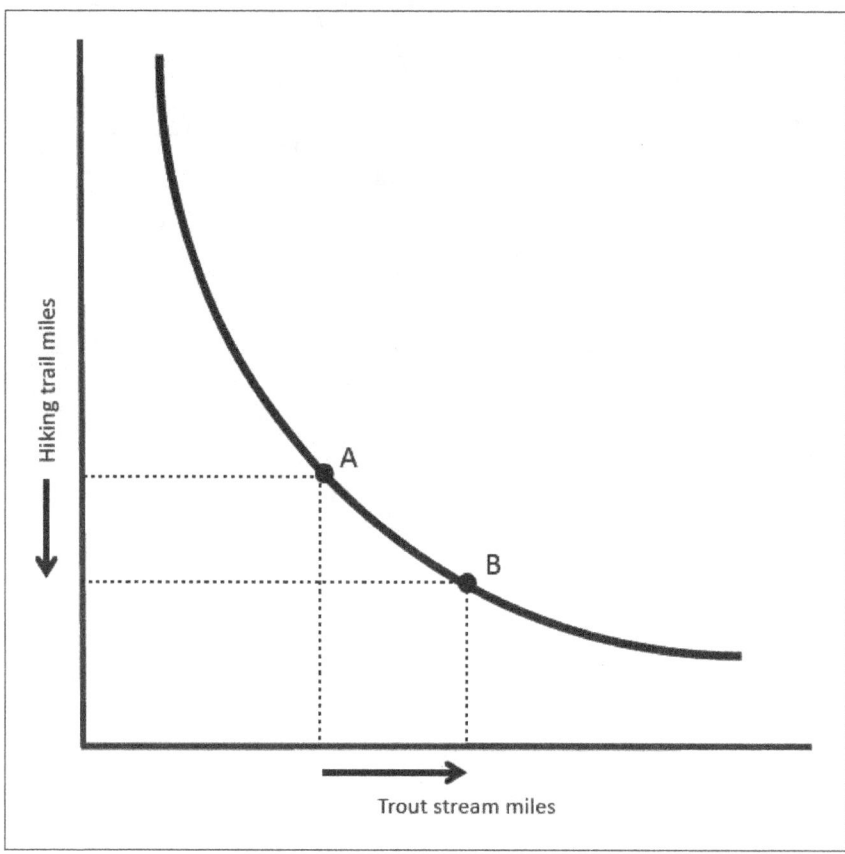

Figure 12—Example of an indifference curve describing preferences for jointly produced combinations of hiking trails and trout streams.

Focus groups, surveys, and other public input can be used to define valved ecosystem services, solicit perspectives on relevant tradeoffs, and assess support or opposition.

trout streams, but the total miles of hiking trails that can be maintained and miles of trout streams that can be restored to prime condition are limited by the landscape and the annual budget. Similar to the way that the shape and slope of the production possibility frontier depicts the nature of tradeoffs necessary in production of two services, the shape and slope of the indifference curve depicts an individual's relative value or preference for two services. The indifference curve describes how much of one service an individual is willing to give up in exchange for another, starting at a particular initial endowment.

For example, starting at point A in figure 12—where hiking trails are plentiful and prime trout streams less plentiful—the hiker might be willing to give up some miles of hiking trails for an additional mile of prime trout stream on the nearby national forest and would be equally satisfied with either outcome. However, starting at point B—where hiking trails are less plentiful and prime trout streams are more plentiful—the same person would sacrifice incrementally fewer and fewer miles of hiking trails for each additional mile of trout stream. That is, they might feel that the quantity of prime trout streams is more than adequate and what they really want is more hiking trails. This concave shape generally is assumed when the incremental (marginal) value of services decreases (is diminishing) with greater and greater quantities available. The slope or steepness of the indifference curve at any given point indicates the general rate of trade or exchange of one ecosystem service for another.

Although this conceptual framing presupposes an economic view of value, it is flexible enough to accommodate noneconomic considerations. For example, there can be points beyond which an individual might be unwilling to give up any additional amount of an ecosystem service in return for any additional amount of another ecosystem service. An example of this might be a case involving a threatened or endangered species. An individual may be willing to accept some decline in, say, spotted owl populations to accommodate some harvesting on national forests, but may be unwilling to allow additional harvest if doing so might contribute to the demise of the species. In this way, economic theory can accommodate factors beyond money and self-interest (e.g., social mores, morals) into analysis of tradeoffs in public lands management by acknowledging constraints on certain uses and the provision of particular services.

Because they are specific to individuals, indifference curves for one individual will not exactly match the indifference curves for another individual. However, by adding up individual indifference curves, it is conceptually feasible to describe a "social welfare function" that is similar to an indifference curve, but for society as a whole (fig. 13). Conceptually, a social welfare function tells us the different combinations of two ecosystem services that are equally preferred or valued by society, as a matter of collective choice. When combined with a production possibility frontier, the social welfare function describes the best combination of ecosystem services from the perspective of society as a whole. That combination is defined by the tangency of the social welfare function with the production possibility frontier (fig. 13), which in our example defines the socially preferred maximum combination of hiking trail miles and prime trout stream miles possible from a given landscape.

In practice, managers usually will lack information about the social welfare function depicting social preferences for the combined production of two or more ecosystem services. However, they may be able to determine the relative values of services over their most likely range of production, using results from a survey of the public, for example. Relative values could be used to compute the negative ratio of the value of one service over another (fig. 14). Similar to the case with a social welfare function, the tangency of that ratio—a straight line—with the production possibility frontier would identify the socially preferred maximum combination of services that could be produced on the landscape over that defined

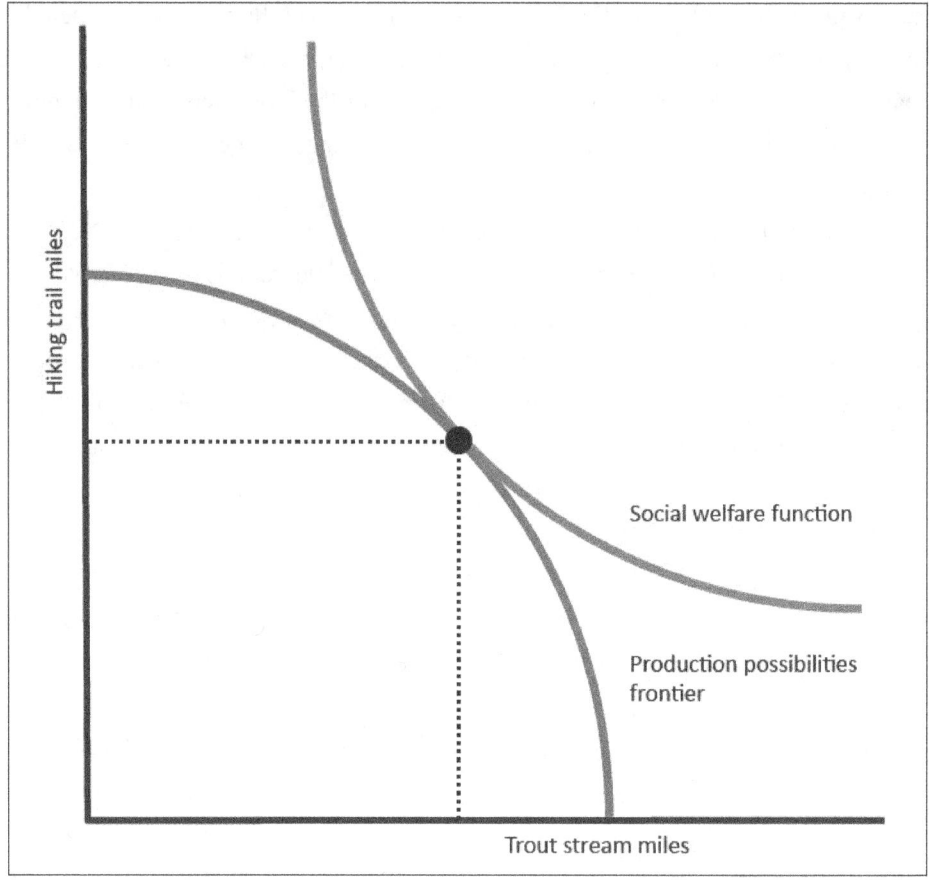

Figure 13—Tangency of production possibility frontier with social welfare function, describing the socially preferred maximum combination of hiking trails and trout streams possible.

production range, given a defined management budget (Stevens and Montgomery 2002). Whether based on a social welfare function or a values ratio, the combination of ecosystem services defined by tangency with the production possibilities frontier identifies that management outcome that makes people as happy as they can be, given the production possibilities available on the landscape. That does not necessarily mean that everyone is happy with the management outcome identified; some people could remain unhappy. This raises the issue of how forest benefits are distributed among the many individuals who make up the public.

Forest management can affect the welfare of individual citizens differently because individuals bear unequal tax burdens associated with national forest management and reap unequal benefits (or costs) associated with management activities. They also have different expectations and beliefs about the purpose of public lands. National forest managers know this well from the public input they receive regarding proposed plans and projects. No proposed alternative will please everyone. In general, all taxpayers bear the financial costs of national forest management.

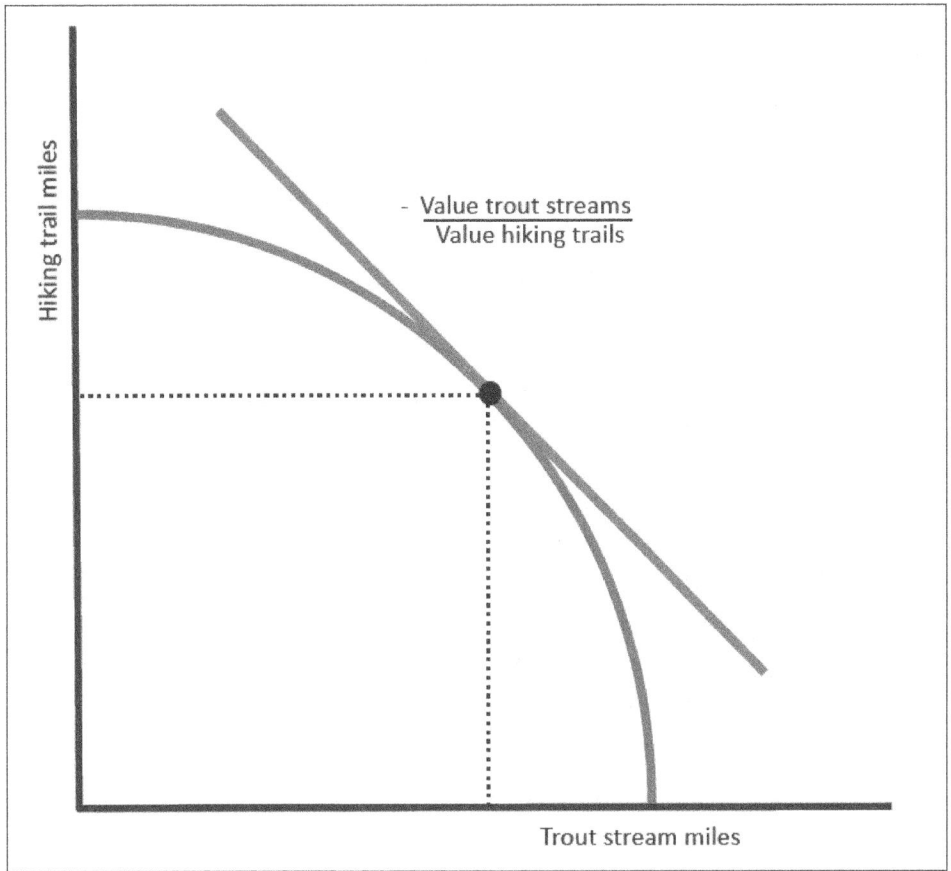

Figure 14—Tangency of production possibility frontier with value (price) ratio, describing the socially preferred maximum combination of hiking trails and trout streams possible.

However, those who gain the most directly from management investments might include people who live near enough to national forests to routinely recreate in them, neighboring property owners whose property values are positively influenced by national forest proximity, and individuals whose livelihoods depend on national forest activities such as timber harvesting and recreation. Other individuals might not gain so directly, but as citizens and taxpayers they also have a say in national forest management. Sometimes, who benefits and who does not can be ambiguous, and will depend on the perceptions and preferences of affected individuals. For this reason, the process of evaluating and communicating management alternatives must include consideration of who might be affected by proposed actions and how. Some benefits will be less well recognized by individuals (e.g., national forests as a source of clean water for human consumption), and managers may need to educate the public about these less-obvious benefits.

Focus groups and surveys of the public can be used to define valued ecosystem services, solicit perspectives on relevant tradeoffs, and assess support or opposition to proposed planning goals or projects (e.g., Asah et al. 2012, Garber-Yonts et al. 2004). They also can be used to develop relative values or preference weights for select ecosystem services to support tradeoff analysis. Particularly useful would be information describing how much of one service people might be willing to give up in return for a gain in other services over the range of changes likely to result from proposed plans or projects.

Whether dollar values are necessary is somewhat uncertain. Although survey research methods developed over the past 30 years by economists and other social scientists have resulted in fairly reliable techniques for estimating dollar values for ecosystem services (e.g., Champ et al. 2003, Freeman 2003), such methods can be expensive and time-consuming to implement. Moreover, recent history suggests that estimating dollar values for ecosystem services has not necessarily improved the dynamics of political and legal processes involving public lands management. We feel that dollar values for ecosystem services are not always necessary or useful for evaluating and describing tradeoffs (text box 2). However, in their absence, ecological information must define key services that people care about in terms that people readily understand (Wainger and Mazzotta 2011). Such information could take the form of benefit indicators (e.g., Boyd 2004, Boyd and Wainger 2002, King and Mazzotta 2000, Wainger et al. 2010). This should be sufficient to facilitate dialog about proposed plans and projects by characterizing expected outcomes in ways that reflect peoples' perceptions about the landscape under management.

From Theory to Application

Evaluating tradeoffs associated with managing public lands can be quite complex in practice. One complication is the sheer number of ecosystem services potentially affected by a given management action and the need to track how each service might change over time and space. It is relatively easy to think about how two different ecosystem services might jointly behave in response to a proposed management action, but it may be more challenging to represent that empirically. Greater difficulties arise when addressing multiple ecosystem services and the interactions among them. These situations typically would require complex empirical models with which to characterize key relationships among landscape conditions and processes and their resulting ecosystem services, including the use of mathematical algorithms and optimization methods to evaluate likely management outcomes (e.g., Stevens and Montgomery 2002). Also contributing to complexity in evaluating and communicating tradeoffs is the inter-temporal nature of forest management effects. Although management costs largely are incurred in the present—the year in which actions are taken—the social benefits that managers might expect to result from proposed actions often occur well in the future. A riparian restoration project today,

Text box 2: Are dollar values necessary?

A common perception that many people have regarding ecosystem services and public forest management is that it is necessary to estimate dollar values for ecosystem services in order for them to be weighed in management decisions. Although values for many forest outputs, such as timber, can be estimated using market prices, values for many ecosystem services, such as wildlife habitat and recreation, involve nonmarket values that can only be estimated using specialized valuation techniques developed by natural resource and environmental economists. The resources available to support forest planning and management may not always be sufficient to estimate nonmarket dollar values. However, dollar values may not always be necessary for evaluating the effects of proposed management plans and projects.

Nonmarket valuation methods have involved varying levels of controversy in their development, which has led to significant refinements over the years. In forestry, the multiple-use mandate of public forests, which occurred simultaneously with the early development of nonmarket benefit valuation methods, stimulated significant interest in valuing resource and amenity benefits arising from forests (e.g., Bowes and Krutilla 1989, Peterson et al. 1988, Peterson and Randall 1984). Today there are generally accepted protocols for measuring forest benefits values and for transferring values to different locations (e.g., Desvousges et al. 1992, Loomis 2005, Rosenberger and Loomis 2001). Prevailing opinion among most economists is that well-designed studies following generally accepted protocols outlined in published literature generally will result in useful information regarding the values of nonmarket forest benefits arising from ecosystem services. Guidelines for measuring nonmarket values are even outlined by federal agencies (e.g., EPA 2000, Office of Management and Budget 2003).

However, measuring nonmarket values for ecosystem services is not without difficulty. It can involve specialized survey methods, such as travel cost and contingent valuation, or benefits-transfer methods based on meta-analysis of past studies (e.g., Champ et al. 2003). These methods can be expensive and time-consuming, and can require specialized expertise to implement. These demands often place nonmarket valuation beyond the reach of public agencies for routine management applications. Also, relative values for different ecosystem services almost certainly change over time. Unless existing databases of nonmarket values estimates (e.g., Loomis 2005, Rosenberger and Loomis

(continued on next page)

2001) are regularly updated based on new studies, they eventually become inaccurate. The Office of Management and Budget recognizes these difficulties in its guidelines for regulatory analysis, and thus acknowledges three categories of benefits and costs of government regulations: (1) those benefits and costs that can be monetized; (2) those that can be quantified but not monetized; and (3) those that cannot be quantified (Office of Management and Budget 2003).

Contrary to an often-stated platitude, lack of a dollar value for a particular landscape attribute or output does not mean that its value enters a given project evaluation as a "zero." Proposed projects should never be evaluated based solely on those ecosystem services for which managers do have good information. Such misuse of imperfect information can lead to biased decisions that favor particular uses and outputs. Rather, managers should compile the best information available about the relevant set of ecosystem services of concern to the public and stakeholders. If relative values in the form of rankings can be obtained, or dollar values estimated, all the better. However, even if managers can only qualitatively characterize likely outcomes, this information can inform a public engagement process that weighs management alternatives through active participation and collaboration by interested parties.

for example, might yield improved fish habitat and greater numbers of fish 5, 10, or more years from now, assuming that unforeseen natural disturbances such as wildfire do not disrupt the restoration process. The further into the future management effects are expected, the greater the uncertainty surrounding that expectation will be. As a result, near-term costs (and benefits) often will trump longer term expected benefits (and costs) in the minds of the public and stakeholders. It is why economists almost always assume some degree of discounting of the costs and benefits associated with expected future outcomes. Uncertainty about the future also is why many economists suggest eating dessert first.

Although complex ecological modeling exercises have been applied to landscape management issues to evaluate an array of spatial and temporal ecosystem services effects resulting from forest management scenarios (e.g., Barbour et al. 2007, Spies et al. 2007), their high cost and time requirements have so far made them impractical for routine application to the work of national forests. Also, to date these types of landscape analyses have tended to limit prediction ability to management effects likely to result from a few select management scenarios, rather than to the full range of production possibilities available. In effect, this leaves the actual production possibility frontier ill defined (fig. 15). Evaluating tradeoffs with more limited ecological information can yield ambiguous conclusions, even with good information about relative values. For example, analysts might be able to simulate two management scenarios that are expected to result in ecosystem services combinations A and B (fig. 15). This would enable analysts to say how much less timber and how many more owls might result from choosing B over A, but that analysis reveals nothing about the numerous other combination opportunities that might exist. For example, it does not inform managers about whether there are other combinations—perhaps a point C—that would allow the same landscape to produce more of both owls and timber, nor does it suggest a set of management activities that could be implemented to move in that direction.

Although characterizing the actual spatial and temporal tradeoffs associated with management activities may be difficult, it may not be necessary to actually describe specific empirical relationships across the entire landscape. At relatively localized scales, particular ecosystem services undoubtedly will fluctuate over time

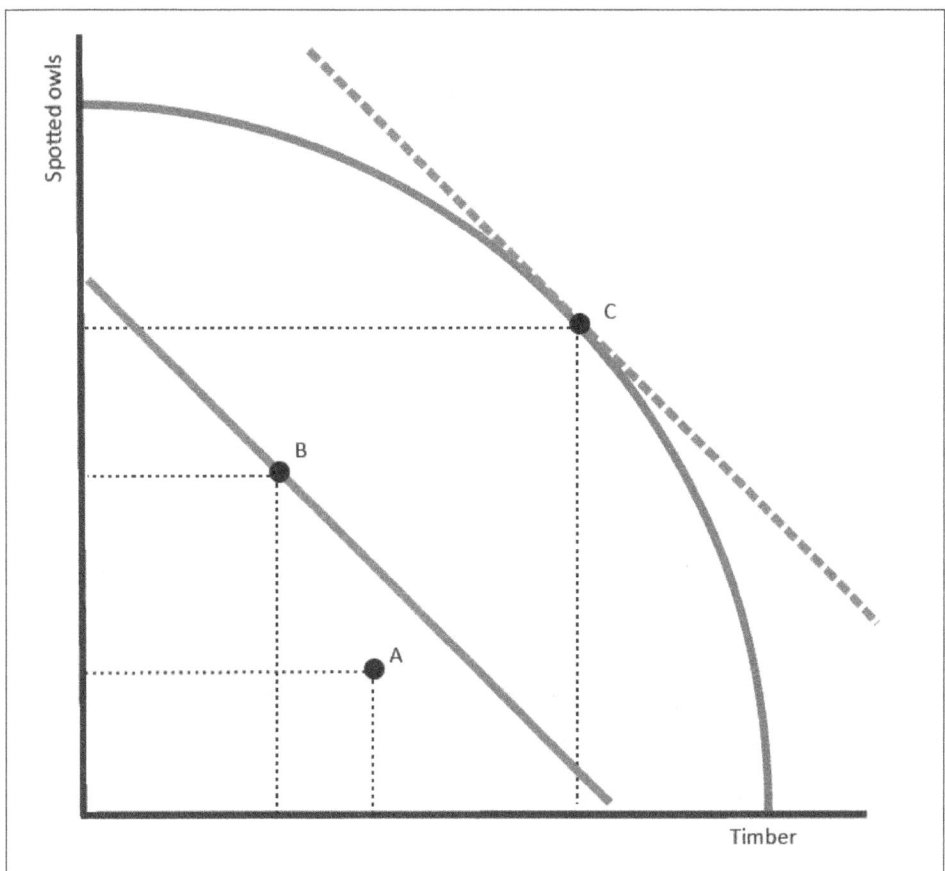

Figure 15—Social preference and its intersection with the production possibility choice set when information is limited. If A and B were the only options we were aware of, B would be superior. However, itf we were also aware of C, that would be superior.

in response to management actions and natural disturbances. However, what may matter more than these localized effects in a national forest management context are the levels of ecosystem services produced from the landscape as a whole—the bigger picture. When management actions and their more immediate localized effects are evaluated, debated, and presented, ideally they would be framed within a larger landscape context with a focus on how local actions and effects contribute to achieving broader landscape-level goals. This is consistent with the conceptual link that defines project-level planning as the on-the-ground implementation of broad landscape goals outlined in national forest plans. It also is consistent with an "all-lands" approach that takes into account the role that neighboring (e.g., private) lands play in influencing ecosystem services produced on the broader landscape. Analysis and communication about management actions during both forest planning and project implementation could focus on describing expected time trajectories of specific ecosystem services as likely outcomes of specific management strategies and actions under consideration, while evaluation of tradeoffs could focus on what the landscape as a whole might produce and how plans and specific projects contribute to those broad landscape goals.

Neither ecological nor social science can anticipate the outcomes that management actions will have on complex ecological and social systems without resorting to some degree of simplification. Still, economic theory offers a rigorous and standardized framework for guiding the evaluation of tradeoffs. Complexity and uncertainty will always characterize this process and at best, only a partial accounting of potential changes in ecosystem services resulting from management may be possible in many cases. However, the fact that information is imperfect does not mean that it cannot be useful in evaluating and communicating the purpose of broad landscape goals and individual management actions. On the contrary, imperfect information may be par for the course. However, national forest managers must recognize and communicate uncertainties that exist in imperfect information. And the Forest Service must give managers the license to do so, by standing behind planning processes and the decisions of managers exercising sound professional judgment in light of persistent but unavoidable uncertainties.

> **Economic theory offers a rigorous and standardized framework for guiding the evaluation of tradeoffs.**

Incorporating Ecosystem Services Into National Forest Management

The process of evaluating and describing forest management outcomes in terms of ecosystem services likely will involve many activities with which national forest managers are already familiar, including:

1. Selecting ecosystem services for analysis, including developing a typology that defines and classifies valued landscape ecosystem services in a way that is relevant to the public and stakeholders; and, identifying the most relevant subset of those on which to focus analysis of likely management effects.

2. Measuring or describing expected management outcomes in terms of the relevant subset of valued ecosystem services, recognizing the ability of the landscape to provide them. This may include ecological analysis and modeling to predict management outcomes, or qualitative description of expected outcomes and uncertainties.

3. Ascribing values or public preferences to landscape conditions and associated ecosystem services. This involves either formally estimating dollar values for relevant landscape conditions and associated ecosystem services, or identifying preference weights to describe the relative value or importance of various combinations of landscape conditions and associated ecosystem services.

4. Evaluating and describing tradeoffs to the public and stakeholders, including making explicit both the ecological and social tradeoffs inherent in pursuing one or another project versus the status quo, and presenting and using some type of selection process to rank, prioritize, or compare the outcomes of alternatives under consideration.

The specific focus, detail, and extent of these activities will differ depending on whether they are conducted in a forest planning or project-level planning and implementation context. Ideally, these steps would be conducted as part of an open and meaningful public engagement process; one that fosters trust among participants that the Forest Service adequately considers their concerns when developing national forest plans and implementing projects.

In the previous section we alluded to various challenges associated with obtaining the information necessary for describing ecosystem services and evaluating tradeoffs among them. Resolving all of the issues involved in meeting these challenges is beyond the scope of this report. However, we will briefly address two primary challenges facing any team embarking on an ecosystem services analysis. The first issue concerns developing appropriate classifications or typologies for delineating specific ecosystem services as benefits of public lands management. The second issue concerns how best to proceed given potential limitations of available data.

Ecosystem Services Typologies

At least since passage of the National Forest Management Act of 1976, natural resource analysts have attempted to develop classifications or typologies for describing the variety of benefits that natural landscapes provide to people (e.g., Bowes and Krutilla 1989: xix). In a national forest example, Randall and Peterson (1984: 38) defined "resources" as the ecological outputs or components of ecosystems that provide valued goods and services, including wood products, water, flood protection, recreation, and various ecological benefits. Their typology included both market and nonmarket goods and services, and is a logical precursor to later ecosystem services typologies developed by Daily (1997) and Millennium Ecosystem Assessment (2005), for example. The more recent emergence of global interest in the ecosystem services concept as a way to inform ecosystem protection and management has resulted in a proliferation of other ecosystem services definitions and classification schemes, with the Millennium Ecosystem Assessment (2005) perhaps garnering the most attention. Although definitions and typologies are widely debated in research literature (e.g., Boyd and Banzhaff 2007, Brown et al. 2007, Costanza 2008, Fisher and Turner 2008, Fisher et al. 2009a, Turner et al. 2008), it is important to understand that virtually any proposed definition or typology usually is intended to suit a particular purpose. This will greatly influence the degree to which any given typology will be appropriate to the needs of public lands management.

Variations among definitions and typologies arise because different individuals and organizations tend to characterize ecosystem services in ways that serve their specific context or purpose, whether it is environmental advocacy, developing environmental markets, green accounting, or public lands management. For this reason, a definition or typology intended to serve one context or purpose will not necessarily be appropriate to another context or purpose. A key way in which typologies differ is in the precision with which they define individual services for possible measurement. Ecosystem services typologies can be viewed as existing along a spectrum characterized by the degree of required precision, which makes them appropriate to different contexts and purposes (fig. 16). For example, a typology intended primarily to support rhetorical argument in favor of greater ecosystem protection can be relatively imprecise (and even vague) in its classification of individual services. The intent might simply be to provide a general listing of benefits that people receive from nature. At the other end of the spectrum are typologies intended to support cost-benefit analysis or an environmental counterpart to gross domestic product (GDP), for example, where greater precision is necessary to avoid ambiguity and potential double counting of benefit values (fig. 16).

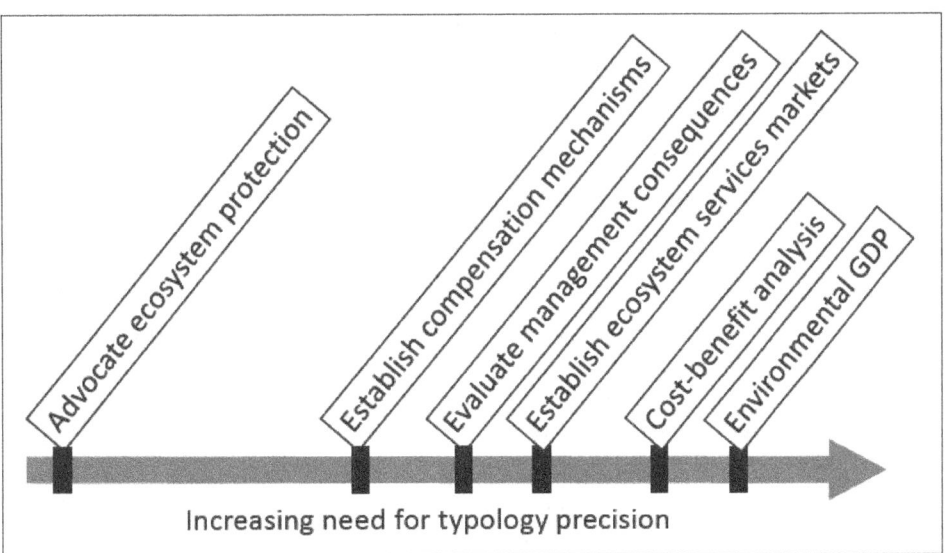

Figure 16—Typology precision spectrum based on intended uses. GDP = gross domestic product.

Published examples of typologies exist all along the precision spectrum. Tending toward the advocacy side of the spectrum is Daily (1997) and the widely cited Millennium Ecosystem Assessment (2005), which in recent years have helped to bring the concept of ecosystem services to the forefront of environmental and natural resource policymaking. The Millennium Ecosystem Assessment (2005) typology proposes a comprehensive itemization of individual services within four general categories: supporting, regulating, provisioning, and cultural services. Although appealing as an organizational framework, many of the individual services identified within these general categories are either ambiguous or simply not amenable to measurement (e.g., inspiration). Other services are double counted. For example, many of the services listed as "regulating services" (e.g., air quality regulation, erosion regulation, water purification) and "supporting services" (e.g., soil formation, photosynthesis, nutrient and water cycling) are actually intermediate services that are necessary for producing virtually any of the final services listed as "provisioning" (e.g., food, fiber, fuel, etc.). As intermediate services, their value or worth would be accounted for by evaluating provisioning services alone. Although useful for initiating policy discussions about ecosystem protection, the imprecision of the Millennium Ecosystem Assessment (2005) typology makes it less appropriate for contexts calling for actual measurement.

At the other end of the precision spectrum are typologies such as Boyd and Banzhaff (2007) and Boyd and Krupnick (2009). These focus on developing ecosystem service measures as an environmental component (or counterpoint) to GDP. In this context, ecosystem services measures must be comprehensive so as to include everything of value, but also must be very precise to avoid any double counting.

Boyd and Banzhaff (2007) and Boyd and Krupnick (2009) thus focus on defining **final** goods and services, as distinguished from **intermediate** goods and services, which contribute to the production of final goods and services. For example, clean water can be a final service when part of a municipal water supply, but also an intermediate service that contributes to the health of a salmon population. Any accounting of water quality as an ecosystem service would necessarily focus on its role in the municipal water supply and would exclude its contribution to salmon, because the later already would be included in an evaluation of the salmon population as an ecosystem service. Final services are biophysical features, quantities, or qualities that require little further translation to make clear their relevance to human well-being (e.g., Boyd and Krupnick 2009: 5, 10). This level of precision is a worthy ideal to strive for in definition and measurement. However, such refined typologies typically will be impractical in landscape management contexts, because the detailed information necessary for characterizing every final good and service and its production simply will not be available. Moreover, in many cases, the requirement that measurement be limited to only final goods and services is unnecessary, because measures of intermediate services often can provide adequate management endpoints for landscape managers when information is limited.

The degree of precision appropriate for characterizing the landscape benefits in the national forest management context is likely somewhere in the middle, though managers should be encouraged over time to strive for greater precision rather than less. Although the Millennium Ecosystem Assessment (2005) typology is often cited in Forest Service publications (e.g., Collins and Larry 2077, Smith et al. 2011), its usefulness as a basis for landscape management arguably is limited if precise economic valuation of final services is desired. (e.g., Fisher et al. 2009b, Fisher and Turner 2008, Kline 2006, Smith et al. 2011, Turner et al. 2008, Wainger and Maz-zotta 2011). Too many listed "services" are too vaguely defined to enable measurement, and too many services tend to double count other services. At the same time, national forest managers likely do not need a comprehensive accounting of all benefits, and in most cases would lack sufficient data to provide such an accounting anyway. Rather, managers might need only an accounting of those select landscape conditions and associated ecosystem services most affected by proposed management actions and that are most valued or of most concern to the public and stakeholders. These could be identified through public engagement processes to identify relevant ecosystem services reflecting the landscape in questions and values people hold for it (e.g., Smith et al. 2011).

The EPA (2006) defines ecosystem services as "outputs of ecological functions or processes that directly or indirectly contribute to social welfare [people]." This treatment of benefits is generally consistent with analytical methods such as cost-benefit analysis, which have been used in federal policymaking and public lands management for decades. Similarly, an appropriate benefits typology to support public lands management would provide enough detail to enable clear distinctions among valued landscape conditions, but be general and flexible enough to enable measurement using readily available or easily obtainable data. In national forest and project-level planning and implementation contexts, a benefits typology might best be tailored to landscape conditions characteristic of individual national forests. However, it also may be advantageous for the Forest Service to define a nationally consistent process for developing ecosystem services typologies in forest planning rules.

An obvious challenge that can arise in developing typologies of valued landscape condition and ecosystem services on a given national forest is the possibility for disagreement among the public, stakeholders, and managers regarding the relative worth or importance of specific landscape conditions and ecosystem services. For example, one group might value trails for off-road vehicles and suggest this as an important landscape attribute to include in a national forest's typology of benefits. Another group may have an affinity for pristine wilderness free of any human incursion and not view off-road vehicle trails as appropriate. The seeming polarity in the interests of different groups can create opportunities for tension to arise in the development of ecosystem services typologies. This may be most appropriately addressed by including a comprehensive set of valued services—including potentially competing values—in any characterization or evaluation of benefits and tradeoffs.

A somewhat related issue—and one more problematic in terms of agency credibility—is the potential duality of factors available to support management decisions, comprising (1) those factors that stakeholders or the public are concerned about, and (2) those factors that managers or scientists believe stakeholders and the public **should be** concerned about. For example, suppose that managers and scientists see a need to restore riparian areas by excluding all recreational uses in order to protect and enhance habitat for a rare or endangered snail—perhaps its protection is even required by law. Managers and scientists might argue for including snail habitat in the ecosystem services typology. However, various members of the public and some stakeholders may not share this same concern, object to the exclusion of recreational uses, and not agree that snail habitat be part of any typology. The best science available will not matter if it is not relevant, meaningful, or believable to the public. Managers often must juggle these competing management expectations, recognizing that they cannot ignore public perceptions and opinions, but also cannot ignore scientific information that the

In national forest contexts, a benefits typology might best be tailored to landscape conditions characteristic of individual national forests.

public may not be privy to, may not agree with, or may not understand. Effectively addressing and resolving disagreements arising from disparate perspectives and perceptions of scientific information is a necessary part of the job of public lands management. In some cases, that process may involve educating the public and stakeholders about why particular factors either should be or must be considered when evaluating proposed management actions.

Another way in which the delineation of describing ecosystem services can differ is the degree to which any defined ecosystem service can be separated from human interaction with it. Ecosystem services typically are biophysical things and many of them can be defined and evaluated using strictly biophysical measures, such as cubic feet of timber, number of fish, acre-feet of water, for example. In these cases, the metrics used to describe ecosystem services are sufficient if they are meaningful to people in the context in which a given ecosystem service is valued, be it harvesting timber, securing a threatened fish population, or supplying a municipality with drinking water. However, in other cases, peoples' perceptions of and values for ecosystem services are influenced by how people interact with them. In these cases, evaluating ecosystem services can involve measures that character-ize peoples' interactions with biophysical landscape conditions, such as hiking trail miles, snowmobile trail miles, and acres of wilderness. Measuring these types of services involves understanding how different people interact with particular ecosystem services and how those interactions might differ from one individual to another, and possibly interact with each other (e.g., cross country ski trails versus snowmobile trails).

Recreation-related ecosystem services in particular are not always neatly linked to a few biophysical metrics, because recreation often depends on diffuse and varied sets of landscape conditions that can differ both by type of recreation activity and by the preferences of individual recreationists. For example, a hiking trail might feature varied topography, open forest, and the possibility of viewing wildlife, a waterfall, or panoramic vista along the way. A trout stream might feature adequate access for anglers, appealing scenery, and riparian conditions amenable to trout, such as cool temperatures, gravel substrate, and varied current. However, recreationists' prefer-ences for recreation-related ecosystem services also will differ depending on the nature of individual uses and preferences. Some hikers prefer quiet wilderness while others are satisfied with even the most congested of popular trails. Some anglers desire pristine conditions while others are less discerning as long as they are able to catch fish. Whatever typology is used to delineate ecosystem services should encom-pass the relevant diversity of uses and values for ecosystem services to ensure that it is meaningful to people and stakeholders who experience management outcomes.

Information Needed for Describing Tradeoffs

Another important step in evaluating forest management tradeoffs is characterizing how valued ecosystem services are likely to change in response to management activities under consideration. This step arguably is more important than placing dollar values on ecosystem services, because value estimates are of little use in the absence of information describing the expected outcomes of management. Ideally, analysis of the likely outcomes of landscape management would be based on credible scientific information linking expected changes in ecosystem services to specific changes in landscape conditions and processes resulting from proposed plans and projects. The quantity and quality of scientific information available for evaluating management effects in this way can differ depending on how well particular ecosystem processes are understood and how well they can be described by ecologists and biophysical scientists as changes in ecosystem services.

In some cases, the state of knowledge about an individual ecosystem service may enable empirical prediction and description of changes likely to result from proposed plans or projects. For example, many economists refer to a need for **ecological production functions** (e.g., Polasky 2008) that link the production of a given ecosystem service in space and time to landscape conditions and processes necessary to its production. Empirical relationships characterizing expected changes in ecosystem services are likely based on a lengthy process of scientific inquiry that has resulted in a widely accepted understanding of the relationship between specific landscape conditions and processes and an ecosystem service that derives from them. In other cases, the state of knowledge about an individual ecosystem service may be less well developed and enable only a best guess estimate or qualitative description of what scientists think might happen as a result of a proposed plan or project. Such variation in the types of data available for evaluating and describing ecosystem services is unavoidable in forest management.

Whether dealing with empirical data and models or qualitative data and narratives, evaluating and communicating expected management outcomes calls for managers to (1) identify key landscape conditions that affect the quantity and quality of valued ecosystem services; (2) characterize key relations between those landscape conditions and the levels of ecosystem services produced; and (3) describe the degree of uncertainty in the data and models used to predict management outcomes. This process includes describing the spatial and temporal aspects of expected outcomes. For example, with a proposed riparian restoration project, the public and stakeholders may want to know how soon and over what area proposed restoration activities are likely to increase fish numbers or yield water quality improvements, as well as how long those improvements are likely to last. Especially useful is information that enables quantitative or qualitative description of how one ecosystem service might vary with increases or decreases in other services—the information needed for describing tradeoffs.

In the absence of good information, professional judgment may be necessary to at least define whether the potential relationship between two ecosystem services is complementary, competitive, or unrelated, and also whether it is expected to be linear or nonlinear and likely to include turning points or thresholds. In these cases, characterizing likely management outcomes may tend more toward the use of simple tables, graphics, or narratives. For example, known or hypothesized relationships among select ecosystem services of interest might be presented in a simple matrix with a "+" symbol denoting a positive relationship, a "-" sign denoting a negative relationship, a "0" denoting no known or hypothesized relationship, and a "?" denoting conflicting information or hypotheses (table 1). Additional symbols could be used to note the strength or magnitude of a hypothesized relationship— three plus signs for a strong positive relationship; one negative sign for a weak negative relationship, for example. Similarly, graphical representations of the expected shape of the functional relationships may be presented. Sets of tables might be used to illustrate how conditions are expected to differ over time and space. Simple descriptions obviously do not capture the complexity in landscape conditions and processes. However, comprehensive simulation of likely management outcomes often is not possible, nor is it always necessary or appropriate for engaging the public and stakeholders in management decisions.

> **In the absence of good information, professional judgement may be necessary to define potential relationships between ecosystem services and management.**

Table 1—Example table showing direction and magnitude of hypothesized relationships between ecosystem services for a given landscape

Service (units)	Timber	Stored carbon	Water quality	Spotted owls	Hiking
Timber (cubic feet harvested/year)		?	- -	- - -	- -
Stored carbon (tons)			+ +	+ + +	+ +
Water quality (temperature)				+	0
Water quality (temperature)					+ +
Hiking (visitor days/year)					

Note The table is for illustrative purposes only and does not imply the nature of actual relationships between specific ecosystem services listed. Gray shading indicates areas on the form that are deliberately left blank.
"+" denotes a positive relationship.
"-" denotes a negative relationship.
"0" denotes no known or hypothesized relationship.
"?" denotes conflicting information or hypotheses.

Ideally, managers would evaluate and describe all of the beneficial and detrimental outcomes likely to transpire over time and space as a result of management actions under consideration. These outcomes would then be evaluated using appropriate approaches. Two approaches that are commonly used to evaluate management outcomes are cost-benefit analysis and cost-effectiveness analysis. Cost-benefit analysis weighs both financial and nonfinancial benefits and costs over time to determine the net social benefits expected to result from a given action. It often is used to rank projects to determine funding priorities. Cost-effectiveness analysis determines the least costly way to achieve a specific objective or, alternatively, the return per dollar spent in terms of outputs produced. Cost-effectiveness analysis is most appropriate when different project alternatives each address the same purpose and need, and the mix of ecosystem services effects expected from each alternative is roughly the same. The choice of approach depends on the degree to which alternatives under consideration might put the landscape on entirely different ecological trajectories with significant differences in resulting ecosystem services flows.

As with information describing production of ecosystem services, data for characterizing the values or preferences that people hold for specific ecosystem services also might be limited. However, it still is useful to consider the degree of importance with which people view particular services and how they might weigh the acceptability of different outcomes. This begins with identifying the basic relationship between valued ecosystem services in terms of human uses or preferences. For example, are two services viewed by the public or specific users as substitutes, complements, or unrelated? It also includes identifying how much of one service people are willing to give up (or exchange) for more of another. Such information can at least provide a general indication of relative value, which is the minimum information necessary for evaluating tradeoffs. We stress, however, that managers should not worry too much about estimating values or preferences for expected changes in ecosystem services until they are first able to adequately describe those expected changes. There is little need for trying to understand values or preferences for proposed management outcomes if managers are unable to adequately describe what those outcomes might be.

Evaluating tradeoffs thus may also often take the form of a narrative of how forest management alternatives are likely to affect the forest landscape and why particular outcomes are desirable to different groups of people with a variety of perspectives. Narratives must describe expected outcomes such that the public and stakeholders can understand the likely benefits and costs of proposed actions, as well as how those benefits and costs are distributed among different people.

Narratives might focus on commonsense factors that are grounded in ecological and economic theory so that professional judgments are reliable and trustworthy. The manner in which information is presented may matter more than its limitations, as long as managers are candid about those limitations and sensitive to the concerns of the public and stakeholders. Managers can begin by asking the questions: What information is available and how can it be presented in a sound and useful way? How can professional judgment be applied in an adaptive and collaborative management process that recognizes peoples' concerns as well as ecosystem integrity and forest health?

Policy Implications

A hope within the Forest Service is that the concept and language of ecosystem services will help managers evaluate and describe the ways in which national forest management benefits the public—as part of an open and meaningful public engagement process. However, in addition to introducing ecosystem services concepts, the promise of adaptive management relies on building a record of outcomes on which to base management adaptations. Therefore, managers also will need adequate resources for monitoring landscape conditions over time, to verify that actual outcomes are close to expected outcomes, as landscapes respond to implemented plans and projects. Incorporating ecosystem services into public lands management thus involves implementing a comprehensive strategy for evaluating, describing, and monitoring the outcomes of management over time and communicating those to the public in ways that welcome meaningful public input. Several actions can help in this process:

1. Support research collaborations among economists, social scientists, and managers to examine how the public and stakeholders perceive and describe forest benefits in their own words. Such inquiry is necessary to develop appropriate benefit typologies for evaluating and communicating expected management outcomes. This includes examining whether ecosystem services language is an effective way to communicate the benefits and tradeoffs associated with national forest management. There has been little research indicating that ecosystem services terminology is an effective way to describe the benefits of national forest management. In fact, existing studies we are aware of (e.g., Metz and Weigel 2010) suggest that, while people understand and are interested in protecting various benefits provided by nature, the term "ecosystem services" is neither well-understood nor particularly appealing to many people. Initial research effort might focus on

Incorporating ecosystem services into public lands management involves implementing a comprehensive strategy for evaluating, describing, and monitoring the outcomes of management over time and communicating those to the public in ways that welcome meaningful public input.

identifying what factors resonate with the public and what words the public uses to describe them.

2. Support collaborative research among economists, social scientists, ecologists, and managers to develop "public-friendly" metrics for describing forest benefits. Metrics should define biophysical characteristics, quantities, and qualities that require little further translation to make clear their relevance to people (e.g., Boyd and Banzhaf 2007, Wainger and Boyd 2009, Wainger and Mazzotta 2011). The likely responses of these metrics to different types of management actions should be understood, as should their relationship to metrics describing other forest benefits, so that joint production relationships can be described. All of this is the essential information for evaluating and communicating tradeoffs associated with management actions, as well as monitoring resulting outcomes.

3. Support collaborative research among economists, social scientists, ecologists, and managers to develop analytical frameworks and decision processes that explicitly incorporate uncertainty and risk in describing forest benefits. This would facilitate collaborative deliberation about management actions informed by the best available science combined with best professional judgment. It could include formalizing adaptive management procedures to guide mid-course corrections as management outcomes become evident over time. It also could incorporate precautionary principals and safe minimum standards approaches to explicitly account for critical uncertainties and maintain viable options for the future, when potentially irreversible changes might result from management actions under consideration.

4. Provide guidance to national forest managers about how to address uncertainty that arises from a lack of information. Increased funding for monitoring, and collaborative research focused on characterizing forest benefits would help to improve the quantity and quality of scientific information available for describing management outcomes.

5. Continue to find effective ways to communicate with members of the public and stakeholders about national forest planning and projects, and to involve them in deliberative or collaborative decisionmaking processes. This includes continuing to ensure that national forest and project-level planning and implementation processes and documents are accessible and understandable to the public and stakeholders, that national forest goals and mandates are clearly stated, and that the quality and limitations of any analyses conducted in support of proposed projects are explained.

These actions will not resolve all of the challenges involved in evaluating and characterizing forest benefits. One persistent difficulty will be reconciling local interests with national interests. Another will be the continued tendency for management opponents to sometimes focus on a narrow range of services or resource outputs, or to simply oppose all actions out of hand. Improved decision frameworks and information may not be particularly useful when perceptions are hardened to scientific persuasion. Presenting information more effectively might help if an impasse involves information and how it is interpreted or understood. However, if an impasse arises from a difference in world views about what public lands are for, better information will not always help. Inviting potential opponents into the management process early might help to defuse potential conflict by enabling people to voice complaints upfront and thereby gain a stake in and ownership of the decision process. Given its complexity in application, characterizing the benefits of public lands management and associated tradeoffs will remain an imperfect exercise involving combinations of conceptual, empirical, and qualitative analysis. However, this is consistent with how difficult decisions often must be made, using professional judgment based on the best information available combined with public and stakeholder input.

Acknowledgments

Partial funding for this report was provided by the Ecosystem Services Team, Pacific Northwest Research Station, Portland, Oregon. We thank Susan Alexander, John Allen, Stanley Asah, Jamie Barbour, Karen Bennett, Dale Blahna, Bob Deal, Krista Gebert, Rickard Hokans, Thomas Mafera, Chris Miller, David Seesholtz, Nikola Smith, and Tom Spies for helpful discussions and comments.

References

Alston, R.H. 1979. Economic tradeoffs of multiple-use management. In: Hook, D.D.; Dunn, B.A., eds. Proceedings of the symposium on multiple-use management of forest resources. Clemson, SC: Clemson University, College of Forests and Recreation Resources: 162–185.

Apple, D.D. 2000. The Forest Service as a learning organization. Washington, DC: U.S. Department of Agriculture, Forest Service. http://www.fs.fed.us/publications/policy-analysis/fs_learning.html. (July 29, 2011).

Asah, S.; Blahna, D.J. 2012. Involving forest communities in identifying and constructing ecosystem services: Millennium Assessment and place specificity. Journal of Forestry. 110(3): 149–156.

Barbour, R.J.; Hayes, J.L.; Hemstrom, M.A. 2007. The Interior Northwest Landscape Analysis System: a step toward understanding integrated landscape analysis. Landscape and Urban Planning. 80: 333–344.

Baumol, W.J.; Bradford, D.F. 1972. Detrimental externalities and non-convexity of the production set. Economica. 39(154): 169–176.

Bowes, M.D.; Krutilla, J.V. 1989. Multiple-use management: the economics of public forestlands. Washington, DC: Resources for the Future. 357 p.

Boyd, J. 2004. What's nature worth? Using indicators to open the black box of ecological valuation. Resources. 154: 18–22.

Boyd, J.; Banzhaf, S. 2007. What are ecosystem services? The need for standardized environmental accounting units. Ecological Economics. 63: 616–626.

Boyd, J.; Krupnick, A. 2009. The definition and choice of environmental commodities for nonmarket valuation. Discussion Paper RFF DP 09-35. Washington, DC: Resources for the Future. 57 p.

Boyd, J.; Wainger, L. 2002. Landscape indicators of ecosystem service benefits. American Journal of Agricultural Economics. 84(5): 1371–1378.

Brown, T.C.; Bergstrom, J.C.; Loomis, J.B. 2007. Defining, valuing, and providing ecosystem goods and services. Natural Resources Journal. 47(2): 331–376.

Brown, G.; Patterson, T.; Cain, N. 2010. The devil in the details: non-convexities in ecosystem services provision. Resource and Energy Economics. 33(2): 355–365.

Buckman, R. 2010. Personal communication. Former Deputy Director for Research, USDA Forest Service, Pacific Northwest Research Station, 3200 SW Jefferson Way, Corvallis, OR 97331.

Champ, P.A.; Boyle, K.J.; Brown, T.C. 2003. A primer on nonmarket valuation. Boston, MA: Kluwer Academic Publishers. 576 p.

Collins, S.; Larry, E. 2007. Caring for our natural assets: an ecosystem services perspective. Gen. Tech. Rep. PNW-GTR-733. Portland, OR: U.S. Department of Agriculture, Forest Service, Pacific Northwest Research Station. 11 p.

Costanza, R. 2008. Ecosystem services: multiple classification systems are needed. Biological Conservation. 141(2): 350–352.

Daily, G.D. 1997. Nature's services. Washington, DC: Island Press. 392 p.

Desvousges, W.H.; Naughton, M.C.; Parsons, G.R. 1992. Benefits transfer: conceptual problems in estimating water quality benefits using existing studies. Water Resources Research. 28(3): 675–683.

Fisher, B.; Turner, R.K. 2008. Ecosystem services: classification for valuation. Biological Conservation. 141(5): 1167–1169.

Fisher, B.; Turner, R.K.; Morling, P. 2009a. Defining and classifying ecosystem services for decision making. Ecological Economics. 68(3): 643–653.

Fisher, B.; Turner, R.K.; Zylstra, M.; Brouwer, R.; de Groot, R.; Farber, S.; Ferraro, P.; Green, R.; Hadley, D.; Harlow, J.; Jefferiss, P.; Kirkby, C.; Morling, P.; Mowatt, S.; Naidoo, R.; Paavola, J.; Strassburg, B.; Yu, D.; Balmford, A. 2009b. Ecosystem services and economic theory: integration for policy-relevant research. Ecological Applications. 18(8): 2050–2067.

Flores, N.E. 2002. Conservation reconsidered, the economics of natural environments, and our understanding of environmental preferences. Working Paper. Boulder, CO: University of Colorado, Department of Economics. 56 p.

Freeman, A.M. 2003. The measurement of environmental and resource values: theory and methods. Washington, DC: Resources for the Future. 491 p.

Garber-Yonts, B.; Kerkvliet, J.; Johnson, J. 2004. Public values for species and ecosystem conservation policies in the Oregon coast range. Forest Science. 50(5): 589–602.

Gregory, G.R. 1955. An economic approach to multiple use. Forest Science. 1(1): 6–13.

Grumbine, R.E. 1994. What is ecosystem management? Conservation Biology. 8(1): 27–38.

Gwartney, J.D.; Stroup, R. 1980. Microeconomics: private and public choice. New York, NY: Academic Press. 510 p.

Kaufmann, M.R.; Graham, R.T.; Boyce, D.A.; Moir, W.H.; Perry, L.; Reynolds, R.T.; Bassett, R.L.; Mehlhop, P.; Edminster, C.B.; Block, W.M.; Corn, P.S. 1994. An ecological basis for ecosystem management. Gen. Tech. Rep. RM-246. Fort Collins, CO: U.S. Department of Agriculture, Forest Service, Rocky Mountain Forest and Range Experiment Station. 22 p.

King, D.M.; Mazzotta, M. 2000. Ecosystem valuation. U.S. Department of Agriculture, Natural Resources Conservation Service and U.S. Department of Commerce, National Oceanic and Atmospheric Administration. http://www.ecosystemvaluation.org/. (September 26, 2011).

Kline, J.D. 2004. Issues in evaluating the costs and benefits of fuel treatments to reduce wildfire in the Nation's forests. Res. Note PNW-RN-542. Portland, OR: U.S. Department of Agriculture, Forest Service, Pacific Northwest Research Station. 26 p. http://www.fs.fed.us/pnw/pubs/pnw_rn542.pdf. (November 9, 2011).

Kline, J.D. 2006. Defining an economics research program to describe and evaluate ecosystem services. Gen. Tech. Rep. PNW-GTR-700. Portland, OR: U.S. Department of Agriculture, Forest Service, Pacific Northwest Research Station. 46 p. http://www.fs.fed.us/pnw/pubs/pnw_gtr700.pdf. (November 9, 2011).

Krutilla, J. 1967. Conservation reconsidered. American Economic Review. 57(4): 777–786.

Lesser, J.; Dodds, D.; Zerbe, R. 1997. Environmental economics and policy. Boston, MA: Addison Wesley. 751 p.

Loomis, J. 2005. Updated outdoor recreation use values on national forests and other public lands. Gen. Tech. Rep. PNW-GTR-658. Portland, OR: U.S. Department of Agriculture, Forest Service, Pacific Northwest Research Station. 26 p.

MacCleery, D.W. 1993. American forests: a history of resiliency and recovery. Durham, NC: Forest History Society. 58 p.

MacCleery, D.W.; Le Master, D.C. 1999. The historical foundation and evolving context for natural resource management on federal lands. In: Szaro, R.C.; Johnson, N.C.; Sexton, W.T.; Malk, A.J., eds. Ecological stewardship: a common reference for ecosystem management. Oxford: Elsevier Science, Ltd.: 517–556. Vol. II.

Marsh, G.P. 1864. Man and nature. Seattle, WA: University of Washington Press. 512 p.

Metz, D.; Weigel, L. 2010. Key findings from recent national opinion research on "Ecosystem Services." On file with: The Nature Conservancy, 526 East Front Street, Missoula, MT 59802.

Millennium Ecosystem Assessment. 2005. Ecosystems and human well-being: synthesis. Washington, DC: Island Press. 137 p.

O'Connell, P.F.; Brown, H.E. 1972. Use of production functions to evaluate multiple-use treatments on forested watersheds. Water Resources Research. 8(5): 1188–1198.

Office of Management and Budget. 2003. New guidelines for the conduct of regulatory analysis. Circular No. A-4. Washington, DC: Office of Management and Budget. http://www.whitehouse.gov/omb/circulars_a004_a-4/. (October 11, 2011).

Pearse, P.H. 1969. Toward a theory of multiple use: the case of recreation versus agriculture. Natural Resources Journal. 9(4): 561–575.

Peterson, G.L.; Driver, B.L.; Gregory, R., eds. 1988. Amenity resource valuation: integrating economics with other disciplines. State College, PA: Venture Publishing, Inc. 260 p.

Peterson, G.L.; Randall, A., eds. 1984. Valuation of wildland resource benefits. Boulder, CO: Westview Press. 258 p.

Polasky, S. 2008. What's nature done for you lately: measuring the value of ecosystem services. Choices. 23(2): 42–46.

Randall, A.; Peterson, G.L. 1984. The valuation of wildland benefits: a overview. In: Peterson, G.L.; Randall, A., eds. 1984. Valuation of wildland resource benefits. Boulder, CO: Westview Press: 1–52.

Resources for the Future. 2003. In appreciation of John V. Krutilla, 1922-2003. Resources. Issue 151: 2-3. http://www.rff.org/Publications/Resources/Documents/151/RFF-Resources-151.pdf. (March 9, 2012).

Rosenberger, R.S.; Loomis, J.B. 2001. Benefit transfer of outdoor recreation use values: a technical document supporting the Forest Service strategic plan (2000 revision). Gen. Tech. Rep. RMRS-GTR-72. Fort Collins, CO: U.S. Department of Agriculture, Forest Service, Rocky Mountain Research Station. 59 p.

Smith, N.; Deal, R.; Kline, J.D.; Patterson, T.; Spies, T.; Blahna, D. 2011. Using ecosystem services as a framework for forest stewardship: executive summary. Gen. Tech. Rep. PNW-GTR-852. Portland, OR: U.S. Department of Agriculture, Forest Service, Pacific Northwest Research Station. 46 p.

Spies, T.A.; Johnson, K.N.; Burnett, K.M.; Ohmann, J.L.; McComb, B.C.; Reeves, G.H.; Bettinger, P.; Kline, J.D.; Garber-Yonts, B. 2007. Cumulative ecological and socio-economic effects of forest policies in coastal Oregon. Ecological Applications. 17(1): 5–17.

Stevens, J.A.; Montgomery, C.A. 2002. Understanding the compatibility of multiple uses on forest land: a survey of multiresource research with application to the Pacific Northwest. Gen. Tech. Rep. PNW-GTR-539. Portland, OR: U.S. Department of Agriculture, Forest Service, Pacific Northwest Research Station. 44 p.

Swallow, S.K.; Parks, P.J.; Wear, D.N. 1990. Policy-relevant nonconvexities in the production of multiple forest benefits. Journal of Environmental Economics and Management. 19: 264-280.

Teeguarden, D.C. 1982. Multiple services. In: Duerr, W.A.; Teeguarden, D.C.; Christiansen, N.B.; Guttenberg, S., eds. Forest resource management. Corvallis, OR: Oregon State University Press: 276–290.

Thomas, J.W. 1996. Stability and predictability in federal forest management— some thoughts from the Chief. Public Land and Resources Law Review. 17: 9–23.

Turner, R.K.; Georgiou, S.G.; Fisher, B. 2008. Valuing ecosystem services: the case of multi-functional wetlands. London: Earthscan. 240 p.

U.S. Department of Agriculture, Forest Service [USDA FS]. 1992. Ecosystem management of the national forests and grasslands. Memorandum 1330-1. Washington, DC.

U.S. Department of Agriculture, Forest Service [USDA FS]. 2005. 100 years of conservation . . . for the greatest good. FS-819. Washington, DC. 9 p.

U.S. Department of Agriculture, Forest Service [USDA FS]. 2012. National Forest System land management. 36 CFR Part 219. Vol. 77 (68), Monday, April 9: 21162–21276.

U.S. Environmental Protection Agency [EPA]. 2000. Guidelines for preparing economic analyses. Washington, DC. 180 p. [plus appendices].

U.S. Environmental Protection Agency [EPA]. 2006. Ecological Benefits Assessment Strategic Plan. EPA-240-R-06-001. Washington, DC: Office of the Administrator. http://yosemite.epa.gov/ee/epa/eed.nsf/webpages/EcologBenefitsPlan.html. (September 26, 2011).

Wainger, L.A.; Boyd, J.W. 2009. Valuing ecosystem services. In: McLeod, K.; Leslie, H., eds. Ecosystem-based management for the oceans. Washington, DC: Island Press: 92–114.

Wainger, L.A.; King, D.M.; Mack, R.N.; Price, E.W.; Maslin, T. 2010. Can the concept of ecosystem services be practically applied to improve natural resource management decisions? Ecological Economics. 69: 978–987.

Wainger, L.; Mazzotta, M. 2011. Realizing the potential of ecosystem services: a framework for relating ecological changes to economic benefits. Environmental Management. 37(1): 710–733.

Walter, G.R. 1977. Economics of multiple-use forestry. Journal of Environmental Management. 5: 345–356.

Webster's Ninth New Collegiate Dictionary. 1990. Springfield, MA: Merriam-Webster. 1564 p.

www.ingramcontent.com/pod-product-compliance
Lightning Source LLC
Chambersburg PA
CBHW081120280526
45787CB00007B/2912